A ROPE OF VINES

By the same author

THE GREEN HEART (OUP)

TIDE-RACE

THE WATER CASTLE

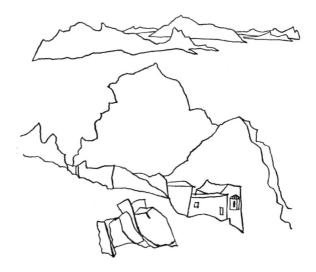

with drawings by the author

A ROPE OF VINES

JOURNAL
FROM A GREEK ISLAND

by

Brenda Chamberlain

HODDER AND STOUGHTON

Made and Printed in Great Britain for
Hodder and Stoughton Limited, St. Paul's
House, Warwick Lane, London E.C.4,
by C. Tinling and Co. Limited, Liverpool,
London and Prescot

AS A GIFT TO YOU
THIS BOOK WITH PRAYER AND CANDLE
I CAN OFFER

I WOULD SHARE HIS SUFFERING WITH HIM
WITHOUT HIS KNOWLEDGE, IN ORDER
PERHAPS TO BE HIS GOOD ANGEL

THOMAS MANN
The Holy Sinner

Also
for Varvara and her child Popi, Anna the gardenia-giver,
Nela of the earrings, Zozo cousin of Nassuli of the felt
hat, Mando the Japanese doll, and other friends at the
Kala Pigadhia

CONTENTS

INTRODUCTION

I have returned to the good mothers of Efpraxia while my friend Leonidas serves sentence for manslaughter of an English tourist in the port of Ydra.

I am putting my thoughts together, for here the mind can clear itself. The nuns ask only simple questions, I have freedom to come and go as I please, no games of pretence are being played as they are every day of the week on the waterfront, I can take a siesta in a juniper tree if I feel like it.

International travellers throw an unreal glamour over the port, but step out of the harbour, and you will come upon club-footed boys, women withering in the sun's luminosity, mal-fed children grossly fat, dwarfs with sun-smitten faces.

A powerful dual reality exists on this island of 3,000 souls and 300 churches. There is a boy in Kaminia who begs for alms running on all fours, his hands calloused from contact with the ground. In the evening, workmen put on their best clothes, and carrying a gardenia between their fingers or gripped between the teeth, saunter into the port for the evening parade along the waterfront.

Where the houses end, the desert begins. Above the desert, on the mountain, is the monasteri.

Since I can do nothing for Leonidas while he is shut away in the prison on the mainland opposite, I am going to see what prayer can do for us both. If living and praying with the nuns leaves Leonidas unmoved and unhelped, then I make my care and prayer an offering to God, from the cell (my flesh) within the cell of plaster and wood, within the cell of the island within the cell of the sea.

From my window in the corridor I can look upon all manner of aerial freedom, so that I long for wings on which to ride over this world of dried-out plants and stone-pines and monasteries, unshadowed and realistic, crazed with cicadas; but the feathers of my wings will have to be strong enough to break the glistening spider's-webs slung from cypress to cypress.

I feel no nostalgia either for the stark town lying exposed at my feet or for the rest of Europe. And yet, though only half-willing to leave this high situation, I am for the battle of the market-place.

The Fates, the inimical forces, will not give me respite.

In the name of God, let me continue to love, and to be loved in return.

For the love of God, let us be made wiser through what we have suffered.

The gods are at war. The air is brittle with thunder and lightning.

I am writing outside my cell, sitting on the wide windowsill from which the wall of the monasteri drops to a small garden of fruit trees. Below the garden, a precipice, under the precipice, the sea. Rain is falling. I find myself surprised by homesickness for my own island when small fishing-boats come into sight, with men standing up in them, as they do in the Enlli craft.

Here, for me, the Welsh sea has joined its fountain-head, the maternal middle ocean that hisses round promontories of pale-boned islands.

The sultry steaming sky is riven by signs and white trees. A mitera passes, trailing a broom.

I have lived for many years in a world of salt caves, of clean-picked bones and smooth pebbles. Towards the end of this period of my life, I began to paint salt-water drowned man, never completely lost to view. They are ledges of encrusted rock, an armoured leg braced in silt, the loins of a body changed gradually into a stone bridge, a wounded torso, flood-tide rising on the walls of a cave into the far corners of which a storm has embedded stones. In particular, there is the breast of the drowned, the man in rock, or the rock-man. A cloud crosses the breast, or a golden light strikes it in shallow water. Detached bones are set in violent motion by storm on the sea-bed.

Now I have surfaced, and it is the light of the world above around in the mittelmeer that fills and nourishes me.

It breaks my heart. Look how other people write. I just glanced at a snatch of Lucretius, copied down in my notebook.

'The moon, night and day, and the stern signs of the night, night-wandering torches and the flying fires of heaven, clouds, the sun, storms, snow, the winds, lightning and hail.'

It must be good to write flowingly and with detachment. It's always by massive bounds and blank pauses, with me. Passion, boredom, despair, flutterings of happiness, memory, and anticipation.

I wish I could write really well, like T. E. Lawrence for example, in certain passages of *Seven Pillars Of Wisdom*, where words became the skin of his adventures in the desert.

I can write. I have a lot to say, but the meaning may not be immediately apparent to more than a few people.

At last, out of this ordered existence, I have thought of a good rejoinder to those who sneer at one for not having a mechanical nine to five job.

'Very well, I'll do your work for six months, and you can write my next book, or paint ten pictures for me.'

PART ONE

THE GOOD WELLS

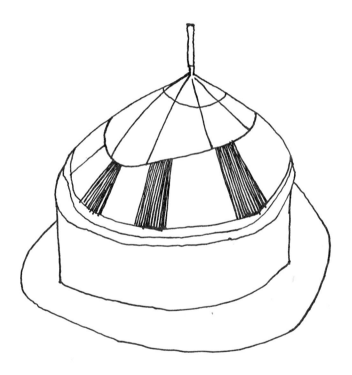

I

A dolphin leapt!
The ship approached a long, thin island of forbidding aspect that looked to be uninhabited until a deep port was suddenly disclosed, surrounded by tightly-clustered white houses against a backbone of rock.

I struggled down the gangplank through the swarm of people fighting to get onto the ship. A man snatched my suitcase and began to run before me through lanes that twisted towards the hinterland. There was no road, only alleyways between the cube-houses that had flat red pan-tiled roofs. We came out onto a dusty track covered in mule-dung, beside a water-course now dry and full of house-refuse.

Somewhere out of sight, in a thicket of prickly pear, a woman gave a warning cry, 'Varvara! Varvara!'

Above wide steps and the two vast wells overshadowed by water-nourished trees, a young woman was standing in a doorway at the head of a flight of stone stairs.

The windows were open so that the air within the house was heavy with the smell of blossom. Lemon flowers, naked mountains, and prickly pear. This is my new house, Varvara will act as my maid. With the help of the lexicon, I ask her where is the nearest shop.

'It is necessary to return to the port for food.'

Varvara took me to the shop of the grocer and of the butcher, and we met a nun of the monastery of Efpraxia. She took me through a blue and white cloister into the church that stands in the middle of the port, and we each lit an aromatic yellow candle before an ikon of the Virgin and Child.

19

Yesterday at this time of afternoon, I was under an umbrella in London, shivering from the grey dampness. And here, it is already summer. I reached Ydra soon after ten o'clock this morning, having come from the Piraeus by the first ship of the day. Mr Dragoumis, not expecting me so early, went to meet the second ship and so missed me, though I met him later on my return to the port with Varvara. He was with another, younger man, also Greek, who had a pale intense face and black curly hair. He was introduced simply as Leonidas. The port and the people in it do not interest me. I am drawn by the monasteries on the barren hilltops. The first thing I must do is to go up there. Is it possible to hire a mule and a guide?

2

Under their iron covers the stone well shafts descended to the water without which the island could not live. Beneath the trees, Varvara and I sat waiting for the mule. Flocks of goats were led past, a bell ringing at each throat.

A party of people on muleback was winding up the mountain-side. Seeing them, Varvara screamed to the donkeyman that we too were coming that way.

A breeze, and heat, and golden promontories. Sitting side-saddle, with Varvara leading the mule, I was nourished by the bald landscape and the scent of herbs. The shaly track twisted and turned between thistles and gorse. We passed a ruined house at the skirt of a wood. A peasant girl came striding out from among the trees, and I wondered whether I would ever have the courage to walk alone on these austere heights.

Coming to the monasteri perched on the edge of a slope, we plunged down a steep flight of steps to an outer yard where the donkeyman, who had gone up the mountain before us, was seated under the shelter of a tree. We shared with him the food we had, a cucumber, an apple, biscuits, and he went into the monasteri for a pitcher of water from the nuns' well.

A nun took us into the inner courtyard, surrounded by cells and kitchens. The courtyard was on two levels, the lower one leading to the cells, the upper one leading to the sitting-rooms, the kitchens, and the guest-rooms. A chapel stood in the middle of the upper level. Rugs and mattresses were hanging out to dry. We were taken into a sitting-room and given quince jam and water. Over the workroom, where cloth is woven, was a low-walled terrace overlooking a valley which was backed by a steep mountain-ridge whose westward slope fell towards the sea. I bought from them a stole, fine white wool run through by a gold thread.

On the way back, we overtook the donkeyman and his cavalcade. We plunged towards the valley with them, a blonde young woman on the leading mule, myself in the middle, and in the rear, an old woman in black. Popi, Varvara's small daughter, suddenly appeared below, having scrambled up the slopes to meet us. She was put up behind the blonde girl and she rode, triumphantly singing, into the top of the village. She was told by her mother to take charge of my animal, but she refused, and ran off defiantly. After Varvara had threatened for long enough, she slipped back and led the animal away, calling out to her grandfather that he should take the mule.

On this island, living up here among the lusty people of the wells, one can forget the souls who wander in the miserable gulf of almost-living, those who are unable to work out the difference between monotony and rhythm. They act under compulsion, at the dictates of a machine-driven existence, when they could know a meaningful pattern of behaviour ordered by the nature of their surroundings. I am thinking of one or two people in particular, of how they like to be driven by the machine because they are afraid to get off and walk or run. The machine rules them in their safe upper-suburban life and for compensation they live more and more in a world of fantasy where they can imagine themselves to be Hamlet, Lear, The Great Lover, The Hero, Artist, Poet. They will never have the courage to try and be what they think they could be. So they make enemies of their families and friends, in order to feel justified in thinking of themselves as rebels against an ignoble fate.

3

I find little reason to visit the waterfront, since each morning, food of one sort or another is brought up and sold beside the Kala Pigadhia, the good wells. Today, the man who brought up my suitcase when I arrived came with a basketful of fresh rockfish. They were silver-scaled, with yellow lines running along the bodies, like the gold threads in my scarf bought from the nuns. They were freshly caught from the night-fishing.

A fat fish with a small pale eye. A broken-handled knife is the only one in the house with any edge to it, so with this I struggled, and found the fish to be more full of muddy slime and guts even than a pollack. While this operation was being performed on the lower terrace, cats appeared from behind the fig-tree and the prickly pear.

Varvara wandered into the garden with her goat and was shocked to find me gutting the fish myself, and surprised that I had done it correctly. She would be more surprised if she knew how many fish I have gutted in my life.

A little later, the baker's boy with a small donkey laden under panniers of fresh bread came by, and I chose a flat round loaf crusted with seeds.

My favourite among these vendors is the old man who shelters from the sun. He is old and wrinkled and almost hidden by a straw hat, from under the brim of which his eyes glance up fearfully at the cruel sky.

In my ignorance I had dreamed of a classical Greece, but in fact, this is already the East, another world than that of Western Europe.

EOKA, in crudely drawn letters, near my house. They tell me that during the war the peasants dropped down dead from starvation. Foodstuffs have to be brought across from the mainland or from other islands.

In a hidden corner near the port, a cooper's shop where wine-barrels of various sizes are being made, some of them large, to which hoops are being fixed with dull blows of heavy hammers.

Within this haphazard clutter of sugar-cube on sugar-cube, it is surprising to discover that so many houses have shady patios with vine-trellises overhead and pots of flowers.

This is an uneasy island, ghost-ridden, and with black danger in the air. It is advisable to keep the well-covers closed at night, for it is possible to have the spirit of a dead person down there, and in the dark hours it is likely to walk abroad if the iron lid is left off. The half-strangled agony of donkey and mule bray makes for uneasiness too, day and night.

4

The animal-train waited in an angle of the bone-white street. A *mitera* with a mischievous face was in the act of mounting her beast, and as she leapt sideways from the wall her body's litheness was clearly evident. Behind her was a laden mule and after, a thick-set *papas* with a grizzled beard sat and kicked his heels into the ribs of the third animal. At the last came a small donkey which the *papas* told me I should mount.

There was the accustomed cry for air from the shuttered white houses piled one above the other on the burnt-ochre rocks. The

papas, who smelt of garlic, held a black umbrella over himself and talked in deep tones with the laughing nun as he gazed round his world of cactus and waterless mountains. We rode past hawk-quartered rocks, through the little pass of the watchtower with its prospect of the sea, to the stubborn track below the turpentine forest. Beyond us white against the sky stood a monastery. A snake, not seen but sensed, crossed our path, while in the air, on high and glittering wires, hung arachne-spinners. Centipedes. Lizards. No sign as yet of scorpions. Praying mantids. A pale green caterpillar with blue-jewelled back. A cicada trying out its voice for summer. A giant saffron-green lizard so startled that it leapt high into the air, over-balanced and landed upside down in a bush on the path below.

In the small whitewashed one-woman monastery with a pencil-sharp cypress tree against a contorted rock and a nimble woman-servant tending a black goat under the pencil-tree, lives this young and beautiful nun who was rich but who gave money and possessions to the church because she had had an unfortunate love-affair. So she decided to punish even God, the black God of incense and incessant prayer, the God of no mercy, by shutting herself away on this red-earthed island in the jade sea of legend where the thistles are miracles of gold. Because she is not seen, she can be imagined as fair beyond the loveliest girls who gather at the well as dawn comes over the mountain-shoulder. In other parts of the world this particular pattern of human behaviour died out or rather was stamped out centuries ago. Here it continues side by side with what we call normal life. The two ways are so adjacent that one can really judge between them, or at least one has the opportunity to make a decision for oneself. I am drawn equally by the two worlds, of the market-place and the *monasteri* murmurous with prayers. Now one, now the other draws me. Whichever one chooses, it leads to a form of self-indulgence. It is only the safe middle way which calls for sacrifice and life-denial.

Facing the matter, seeing it unsentimentally, it does not seem much of any sort of life to imagine oneself translated into the beautiful

27

nun, who to be truly the traditional example must have had high spirits and good, if not positively aristocratic, breeding and either classical or extraordinary beauty, wit, learning, a mutilated heart and a fanatical sense of prayer. Set the woman, the nun who is me as I am her, with a woman's part to somehow employ, to rise at dawn in this land's summer of bright days (a desire to get even with the lover by espousing God) and let her decide, shall she mutter prayers in an airless room while a withered and sharp-practising servant in black weeds has gossip and morning commerce at the wells, or does she, in a house whose doors and windows are wide, clad in nothing but her skin, stretch contentedly, unfolding from a man's arms, her legs released from his, to face the challenging world, the battle that follows each night's truce? It is clear that so great a cleavage in my nature will never be resolved, now a life of withdrawal (I will not call it sacrifice, for it is a form of self-indulgence), now worldliness, both draw and equally. I do not like the idea of the crone-guardian under the cypress-tree. Would she, not God, tend to control a life so close-knit with hers?

5

Opposite my house, at the other side of the wells, lives an English family. They have two children, a boy and a little girl of six with straight bleached hair. The children attached themselves to me, and we went for a walk together up the steps past the weavers' house onto the mountain, looking for snakes and ruins. The boy is intimidated by the strangeness of this environment, but the girl is part of the tough context in which she finds herself. We made for a grove of trees behind a ruined house. The children lagged behind, imagining they could see serpents in every gorse bush and herb-tuft. Here, in the middle of the wild mountain, was a sense of habitation. I called the boy and his sister to come quietly: a cicada was making sad music among the fir trees.

The boy rushed up to say he had seen a phantom.

'A man dressed all in white is there, by the old house. He is standing at the well.'

His sister scoffed, 'There's no such thing.'

I called, 'Come on, there's a good view of the mountain-top from up here.'

The boy was red in the face, and almost in tears.

'I'm going back home. There is a ghost here.'

They began a bitter quarrel about whether there were spectres or not. I remembered how his father had told me he had once before refused to go beyond a certain point on the mountain, somewhere near this ruined place.

Going home, we were greeted before we had reached the outskirts of the town by the long-drawn unearthly wails of the Kala Pigadhia cats, raising up for me too-clear pictures of nimble bodies squeezing through shut doors, jaws opening meat-safes, the unearthly inventiveness of the half-wild animals, busy at our food supplies. As I mounted the steps to the front door, a cat leapt out of one of the windows of the salon into the topmost branches of the almond tree and made its way to the ground with a practised air, a really long way down to the earth.

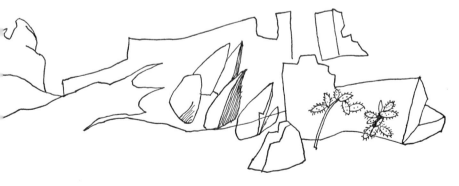

6

Sophia is a sad brown woman with a nervous tic in her face; gipsy-like in features and manner, bone-thin and hungry-seeming, always wearing the same faded garment. She lives with her old mother, and their poultry and cats, in the small house next to the one temporarily inhabited by the Englishman and his wife and children.

Sophia's cottage has been transformed with the maximum of drama and upheaval, in which we at the wells were somehow involved. The noise and passion aroused was beyond belief. A week ago, the Twitch-Sophia received a letter. Full of important good news, it was handed round to many people to be read on the doorsill. Kassandra, a neighbour, was particularly interested.

Two workmen, one of whom was Varvara's husband, arrived to talk the matter over, and the following night, the grandmother's house knew no rest. At midnight under the full moon they sat on the wall under my bedroom window, Kassandra and her spoilt granddaughter Mando, the granny, Sophia, shrieking and threatening one another. No sooner had they gone to bed, it seemed, than it was dawn and they were awake, flinging out the contents of the cottage onto the whitewashed steps. The settle was put for safety against the house-wall, out of the way of donkeys and mules who paced up the steps with loads of cement and plaster and new tiles. The transformation of the 'plumbing' had begun, thanks doubtless to the letter from America. Trouble started between the two women, who raved with hatred for one another. Sophia threw a dustpan at the old one, and threatened to twist her nose, all the while twitching on and off her head covering, finding it necessary to walk away a few yards to cool herself down, crying to the neighbours to listen to the idiotic ideas of the ancient woman who, at one stage of the upheaval, was shut up in a back room, but who for most of the time sat on her chair on a plank over the newly-placed tiles. She would not for one moment give up her position in the house. During this time, the cats, cock and hens had to live outside, but the cock was fed liberally with corn by the old woman. The workmen laughed amidst the battle, but even they were plainly in a hurry to get out and away from the turmoil. When the men had almost finished their work, Sophia began to sweep the cement dust off the steps outside, towards the open door of the house, muttering and moaning to herself.

Kassandra had during the drama deserted her own orderly house and had fed her granddaughter inside the grandmother's house-door.

'Greece's never-ceasing struggle with the powers of chaos.'

As the cement-dust began to settle, the cock stepped delicately back into the house, the cats once more draped their meagre bones along the outside steps. Sophia went to the well with a bucket and a towel, and became absorbed in washing her feet, watched from the shadowy house by an unrepentant and unforgiving mother.

So they now have plumbing, that is, a sink from which the water will almost certainly not run away down the pipe.

This morning, Sunday, there is peace once more at the grandmother's. Sophia smiles again through her twitches, and granny can once more sit outside the door, with the orderly cottage behind her. Shaking dust out of his wings, the cock crows, his confidence restored.

This uneasy truce soon ends, for still at nightfall Sophia makes, at the last possible point of the day, her escape from the house. Here is the daughter's triumph, old age being beaten by stringy vigour of middle age. The grandmother can never grow accustomed to this moment of betrayal, when the daughter walks out into her private affairs. The two women scream at one another for as long as Sophia is within voice-striking distance, then the grandmother continues for her own satisfaction and that of the cats—the words are repeated over and over, her voice deep at first, rising to a sudden sharply screamed curse. She flits back and fore in the small space of her house, to and fro about the dim oil-lamp, while the cats prowl over the table, taking quick snaps at the old one's supper. The crone cannot rest, the strings of her headcloth hang over her ears, a doll's pigtails, and if she hears a footfall on the steps she is out at once to shriek her grief, disgust and bitterness, enough to curdle the reputation of her daughter.

7

The peasants are harvesting wheat in the belts of cultivation terraced high on the mountain-sides. A family party, preparing to go up there, rested awhile under the trees at the good wells. There were two pack-mules, and a man and his wife, a small boy and a baby girl. The girl was in a straw confection of funereal whiteness, a hat an old woman could have worn with propriety. The family enjoyed a good rest under the shade of the trees, then at last it was time to be off. When they came out again into the light, their faces showed black in the intense glare of the sun. The mother leapt sideways onto the first mule, and the girl was lifted into her lap. The father took the boy with him onto the second mule, and the party was off along the steps and away behind the houses toward the mountain.

Popi called for me after school and we climbed through the stifling air to where Varvara and Nassuli's mother had spent the day reaping in the wheat-terraces. For shade, we sat under a holm-oak near Varvara's goat.

Eyes could see so far, it was like looking through a telescope. Near us, a red hawk hunted, and in the rocks at the other side of the gorge, two little owls were quarrelling.

Nassuli's mother was in a dark red dress and a white visored head-cloth. Varvara was in her faded blue frock and over it, as protection against the sun, making her look like a guerilla girl, she wore one of her husband's shirts, torn and faded but clean.

The husk of the grain they were reaping was rocky, dry, and burnt by the sun.

We seated ourselves beneath the tree, and Varvara opened a cloth containing small bitter olives, pieces of cheese, and thick hunks of crusty bread baked by Nassuli's mother.

From the belfry in the middle of the port a bell tolled. Crouched on the powdery red earth and stubble, Varvara crossed herself.

I was awakened before dawn by what sounded like someone having fallen down one of the wells trying vainly to get out, or a house being dismantled. Outside the window, everything was quiet. There was a crash in my kitchen. A cat lifted its head from the yoghourt. It must have taken a leap from the pantiles over the outer gateway to one of the open windows of the salon.

In the almond tree beside the upper patio, a cicada creaks, informing me that the days are drawing towards mid-summer. I come out to look at him, but fail to distinguish him among the leaves. His eyes are better than mine. He falls silent.

An ant passes my foot, dragging a long pink petal.

A lame woman has just led three laden mules and a donkey past the house and up the white steps towards Kiapha. The beasts were hung over with bundles of household gear wrapped in woven cloth of red, bright green, orange and yellow stripes—square bundles, water-pots, a straw hat, carved crooks, a mass of rooted herbs and cooking utensils. A small pale-coloured donkey brought up the rear, carrying dead poultry, two on each side tied by the legs and flopping forlornly their broken necks. Then another donkey with two sack-panniers, each one bearing a contented sheep with foreleg delicately dripping from the mouth of the canvas bag.

8

Varvara has been up to the house to give me a gardenia. Elene, the young wife from next door, is singing a monotonous chant.

It has been cooler today, but what was this morning a breeze is now a wind of warm and powerful gusts coming up the valley from the sea, and it will probably turn into a storm, *meltemia*, such as Shelley drowned in.

From this high-up house, I can look onto the tops of the waving walnut trees and the prickly pear and across the valley to the houses built among boulders, tortuous steps.

The air is full of the threat of thunder. White horses rear on the grey sea. I have been sitting on the opposite side of the gorge, on the balcony outside the house of Varvara's mother. Varvara complained that her mother was so fat because she ate too much. Later, when it was almost dusk, we went to Varvara's house where we had bread dunked in rich sweet chocolate. Popi brought me a nosegay of roses, a white lily, and a sprig of sweet basil from the darkness of a rocky garden. In the yard is a wash-house containing two big wine butts lying on their sides, from one of which Varvara ran me off a bottle of home-made retsina. The wine was harsh, of a strong golden colour and with such a taste as one would expect to come out of this shaly-arid land.

The old mother, save for a long siesta time when the curtain is drawn over the closed door, sits an incubus outside day-long, preying on her daughter below. She is preparing for winter, with raw wool and spindle busy.

9

On our way to the turpentine forest, where the English family and I had decided to spend the midsummer night, we were passed by three mules that had escaped from their stable at the head of the valley. They cantered off to the nearest patch of cultivation, from which they knew the young son of the muleteer would soon bring them away. The air was so clear, the wheat grew so sparsely, that their legs were visible, appearing to be watery shadows abnormally long, gliding between the stems.

We went close by the empty monastery; along its whole extent, it was walled and fortress-strong, with a chapel in the middle, and a big well outside on the mountain. Living like dogs in a kennel at the rich man's gate, a peasant family inhabited the meanest kind of hovel, built to suffer the hot eye of the midday sun. It was a thing of sacking and twigs and tumbledown shelters with sparse bushes round it, on which a woman in weather-faded tomato-coloured dress, was hanging grey rags to dry. A lanky girl was there too, skipping with a tired length of rope her only playmate on the dry, stony earth.

A half-moon lit the wood where we lay on a level space between the trees, each of us rolled in a blanket. The pines were cut and cupped for turpentine, and the smell of resin was overpowering. The air was cool, not cold, and there were neither winged nor crawling insects. In the rocks of the mountain behind us, all night long there was a sound of sheep-bells from the flock that had been let out at dusk from the monasteri sheepfold where the farmer's wife had filled our water-bottle.

Below us, from the sea outside Mandraki, came the sound of engines from the night-fishers' boats.

I slept soundly for the first time in weeks, not sweaty, not bitten by mosquitoes.

In a pre-dawn light, we struggled to wake, and then wandered soul-bereft about the cupped and wounded trees, looking for the morning.

We climbed down onto the path and still half-asleep began to walk in the direction of Zourva and the eastern sky. On the ridge's brink, we sat among rocks and thistles in a slowly-growing grey light. The sea was grey and wrinkled, the thistles drier than ever, pallid. The lower land towards the west was already in a noose of sunlight. There was a farm in the sheltered part of the hill, and it bore signs of cultivation, patches of corn, vines, and a high-walled circular 'garden' of cactus and fig. Below lay the open sea.

The world of men was suddenly abroad, men on mules, a boy in a pith hat riding a donkey. The peasants laughed down at us from their wooden saddles as they rode towards the farm. The sheep were being brought down the mountain.

There were cries, and a distant dust from the threshing floor of the monasteri.

At last, the sun lay golden round our feet, the sky blued. We went back into the pine trees' shade to eat breakfast of hard-boiled eggs and frankfurters, retsina, water, and apricots. It was still cool under the trees, but when we came out into the open again, we realized it would be another 'Touch not the wall' day.

The gateway of Agios Nikolaos was opened by a witch-caretaker. She mopped and mewed round the chapel, pointing through a corner of the eikonostasion at a silver-bound bible heavily chained. There were numberless offerings of silver eyes, and legs, and more eyes, festoons of silver legs.

The doors in the yard were numbered, one with a cat hole at the corner. A terrible convulsion shook one of them, marked number four.

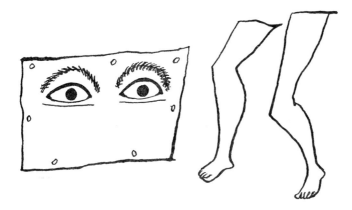

'Good God. A nun wants to get out, she cannot bear it any more.'

The windows are barred, she has been on her knees the whole day in the airless room, and she is going mad to be let out into the thyme-heavy air, she wants to run with the vari-coloured goats among the boulders, to be in the world of dragonflies and cicadas, to perfume her fingers with the sugary white resin bleeding slowly from the pines, to go among the terraces of withered thistle and wire-netting plant loud with grasshoppers down to the bay of Limionisa, and there to lie star-fished on the surface of the buoyant navy-blue sea, gazing half-blinded into the eye of the sun, after throwing her buckled belt and black garments into a mound for exploration by soldier ants.

O God, you unholy, garlic-reeking witch, let out the poor mad nun!

Mopping and bobbing, the witch crossed to the door and let out a small white dog and a lean cat. To show off her pet, to make a circus-turn out of her dog's pleasure in being released, she jumped up and down in the heat-stricken yard. The more the dog disregarded her, the wilder became her cries and gestures. At last, bravo! he barked, and she was convulsed at his intelligence.

She pushed me forward into the room that smelt of decay and

despair, touched by the outside world of politics and war. Photographs and sacred pictures covered the walls. Here was her son killed in Egypt, there was a bridal group. A black dress hung by the closed window.

There was still no sign of a nun.

'It is years since they went away,' mouthed the witch.

By the time we came out, the world had lost its eyebrows in a white-hot wilderness of thistle, stone, and derelict wheat-terrace. The land was the colour of wet salt and there was a beautiful nakedness about the harsh soil. The sea was bare, no other land or island or sail or even puff of distant funnel-smoke marking it. The cliffs and man-made terraces fell away into the red-blue eye of the Aegean, but for a few yards out from the cliff-foot, the water was jade. Where the jade ended, the fire-shot blue began, and continued to the horizon.

The 'cactus garden' was a high stone encirclement, a claim to civilization, the topmost rocks bearded with a fringe of furze as extra protection against the goats. Among the vigorous leaves, bright at their edges with yellow flowers, was one plant gross and fleshy in decay, withered and wrinkled and mutilated, the vegetal equivalent of a dead elephant, hanging grey and lifeless, with broken-boned limbs.

On our way home, at the deserted monasteri, on the sloping ground a young donkey was tethered to the shadow of a carob tree. Through an opaque dust-cloud, we went up to the threshing floor to greet the farmers, while the mules and one donkey went round and round, the donkey nearest the pole, the mules graded by size from the pole out to the tallest beast.

It was not yet hot enough to make us feel that we were in danger of frying on the naked slopes. Smelling of sweat and turpentine and red dust, we came home in silent contentment, each carrying a bedroll, to be greeted like returned travellers from Africa by the women gathered at the wells.

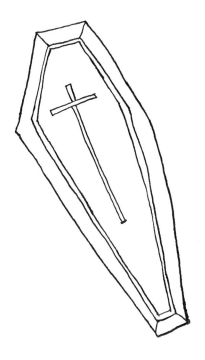

10

A funeral was coming up from the port to the cemetery in the mountain. The corpse was that of an old woman, who lay exposed to view in the coffin, with her hands tied together by a black band in an attitude of prayer. The priest gestured that I should honour the corpse by looking upon it. The coffin lid was carried upright, prominently, like a huge palm leaf.

There it lay, the dry husk of the woman who had been the sybil of Katsikas, she who had sat for years, leaning on a stick, always drunk, watching the passers-by. She should have sat not under the awning of Katsikas, but under an olive tree at a cross-roads, giving advice and warning to the young.

To watch the procession, Sophia had posted herself above her house. Against a background of cacti, with her shadowy face, she looked like a jungle woman.

She shouted, 'Who are they burying?'

The mourners carried the coffin close to the red cave whose mouth is sealed by a gate. I knew they would pass by, but it would have seemed fitting for them to have placed the coffin within the cave.

I I

For good eyesight, God should be thanked each day, a candle should be lit in gratitude to the Virgin.

One evening, at the wells, that time between day and night when the trees seem to have become most full of leaves, two small children with five goats, a brown nanny and her four kids, one black, two white, the fourth white with brown and black spots, came wandering out of a fold in the rocks, ascended the steps, walked about the wells, then quietly withdrew into the hill.

A mule-train six beasts strong, carrying loads of corn, came down from the fertile valley under Ere, and Varvara came into the house smiling, with rubbed ears of grain for us to sample.

1 2

The wild, black-eyed woman who lives in the hovel beside the mansion opposite was singing into a black night and a heaven of stars her grief and despair, strong and inevitable as the fall of waves against the land; a primitive, lost cry of the heart of a savage woman in a poor cottage lost on a Greek island, with endless washing under the tree, her children going to the well for water, no mind or book-learning, only grief marking the night for us so that we throw the doors wide open, throw open another window. She is singing of the sadness of life. This is the mother of Aldo, the boy who bites. Her husband is a drunkard. On this feast day of Ermioni he was lying in the blazing sun at midday on the Kala Pigadhia, his face and white shirt all bloodied. It was the middle of the afternoon before he had succeeded in dragging himself home.

1 3

There are small, round water-vents at the bottom of each window, which end in short tin waterspouts on the outside of the house. One day, while I was leaning at the window, a wild bee winged into one of these vents. This morning, I have discovered most of the holes to have been cemented on the inside of the window by uniform, minute pebbles held together strongly by a green cement, on the outside of the window, at the end of the metal pipe, by a dun-coloured stoneless cement.

14

Black-haired and with a pale oval face, a girl on muleback, followed by a young man and a handsome *papas*, tall as an El Greco saint, both on foot, came down the steps from Kiapha, crossed the wells, and

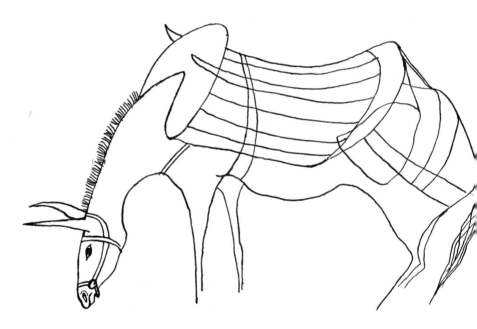

went up the other side of the valley. Later in the evening, I heard a bell ringing from the abandoned monastery, then for the first time I saw lights shining from its long windows. The bell was rung again this morning. At dusk, the three returned in the same order, the girl ahead on the mule, followed by the young man and the smiling *papas*.

This priest is a man of heroic size, who sometimes passes my door, riding a fine black horse, and carrying a red bag. One day when I was on the coast road, I saw him come across the mountain to bathe in a secluded part of the rocks. Leaving his horse to forage at the wayside, he plunged down the slope towards the sea, taking off his black robes as he went.

15

Thank heaven, the Englishman yesterday killed the diseased kitten while the children were out bathing. He came over to my house for a drink of retsina to make him forget what he had in humanity been forced to do. Somebody should come along with chloroform and a gun to destroy almost the whole cat population of the island. It is a nightmare of horror to see so much disease, torn bodies, swollen limbs, eyes hanging out. Most of them should be destroyed, but if they were, then we would be inundated by rats and mice without any doubt. The stone ditch is becoming increasingly noisome in the heat, since every form of garbage is thrown among the rotting cacti. Every so often a child comes out and lights a bonfire which fills the evening air with strangely teasing smells. Gardenia Popi flits moth-like from flame to flame with cries of excitement to encourage the fires.

Just now, a short way above the port, I came upon Zozo, the daughter of Evangelos Limmiotis, an old boatman, sitting on the wall of the Kala Pigadhia, resting with her shopping, a huge dark-green melon. She looked almost cross-eyed with passion for her sharp-featured young donkeyman. I met him near Loulou's, and told him that Zozo was resting further up the street. His features became even sharper. Wordlessly, he hurried away to find her.

On the *agora*, a band of boys, one carrying a long bamboo pole with a cicada attached to its point, pursued a cat from one of the tavernas, thrusting the pole under the tables in hope of encountering the animal, regardless of the people who were dining.

16

The tall mountain pines generate their own strong winds. Whereas a few feet away, out in the sun, the sweat runs down my body, under the breath of this tree, with the mad cicadas screeching among the fir-cones, I could remain cool throughout the day.

O for a goatskin full of retsina, a handful of olives, a cucumber.

The slope falls sheer into a ravine, and on the opposite side, the cliffs are fiery, reflecting the flame-coloured rocks below, invisible to me, except in this reflection.

Below me, a stone's cast under the many-roomed *monasteri*, a short way above the ravine, on an isolated small plateau, is a primitive stone hut, without windows or chimney, a large central doorway, filled with darkness, reaching to the roof. As protection, a low wall encircles it. The paws of the stockade rest a man's width from one another, allowing passage to the doorway. Outside the enclosure, among stones and thistles, stands what appears to be a communal bed of woven straw braced with wood. Women and children move about this primitive dwelling. I dare not go near, for shame of having so much richness about me, cool sandals on my feet, a leather armlet, rings on my hand, of having some kind of lightness while they are pressed down onto the earth by the weight of the sun.

A young *mitera* is riding home at a brisk trot, with full panniers. She shines with a blessed happiness, as well she may, in such a landscape, in such a climate. She has about her a workmanlike air, for she is wearing a faded black tunic, pocketed and girdled, such as an artisan wears. On her head is a yellow straw hat, the brim wide as a cart-wheel, anchored by a black tape tied under the chin.

She urges on her mule with gaiety and merriment, and greets me with freedom. She is riding among the grasshoppers to the safety of the white fortress, followed at a distance by two men carrying laden bread-baskets.

17

To Ermioni, a large proportion of the populace of Ydra, and of other islands as well, went on a sacred pilgrimage this morning. Popi was there with her grandmother, among the assemblage of peasants gathered in the port. Each pilgrim was carrying a long bees' wax candle as well as food for the day and night of vigil. One couple was unlike the run of Ydriots, a tall man and his tall wife, singularly similar in face and figure, both iron-haired and noble-faced, smiling with serenity as they sat at a table drinking lemonade.

On its arrival, the ship seemed to be already full, but the eager candle-bearers streamed endlessly aboard, shrieking and exhorting. In the crush, Popi was carried away from us, pale and petal-faced under a straw hat.

Those left behind on the quayside backed into the foot-wide shadow cast by the tourist shops, raising their arms to the sky in complaint against the heat.

18

A refreshing sound to which I am growing accustomed is the cool swishing that fills the air as peasant women beat with long poles at the boughs of the water-nourished trees between the wells. With raised heads, the goats cluster, to catch the leaves as they fall.

19

The way the mountain people tend their young fills me with wonder. The farmer who goes over into the valley under Ere every Sunday morning (watched by three women, the grandmother in a white head-scarf, his wife in a cool Mother Hubbard) spoon-feeds the deliciously cool, clean child dressed in airy muslin, white socks and shoes, gauzy hat with a stiff brim. The child, a princess, opens her petal mouth to take in the gruel.

As for Mando, she is every spoilt little girl in one, plump and sexy with a round head of sleek black hair, insinuating body, smooth-skinned and plump, and touch-me-not airs, because she knows her mama feels guilty towards her for being so frequently away with her seafaring husband. As for Kassandra, her grandmother, who is chief among broody hens, every affected gesture made by Mando, every petulant denial, every hysterical scream, is registered by the

proud nerves and gives food for anguish. Mando at four years of age is the apotheosis of the sex kitten.

Intelligent children of five are still being spoon-fed like small babies and they scream loudly before they will submit to having the food put into their mouths.

20

The light is honey, clearest gold. The ruined walls of ghostly Kiapha on top of the cliff are transparent and most golden when the sun is going down behind them and they are actually in shadow. They reflect the light still beating strongly on the white houses of the opposite side of the mountain. The yellow-ochre mansion opposite my house casts much of this light on the cliffs, the cacti, the grasses, and the ruins of this side of the mountain, for though our side loses the sun as it westers, the mansion, still brightly-lit, acts as a mirror to these things.

21

I found a track immediately opposite the house, a path that twisted and turned in its narrow shale bed, rising precipitously between pale thistles. Having rounded the rocky corner into the next valley, I came upon another, but another miraculous landscape, the earth a sultry, almost purple red, tall ear-full corn, olive trees, a meandering path under fir-trees, giving sudden savage glimpses of naked, grey outcrops of the Koundaria. A few half-ruined buildings stood among the olives. Two magic trees stood a little apart from the more sober ones. Among bright-green, glossy leaves, their flame-coloured flowers were already half-way to becoming fruit. In this hyper-clear air, the red-hot earth showed between each pale stalk of corn. This was another, a totally other land from the inhabited side of Ydra, fertile, wooded, corn-terraced, a more tender world of trees rooted in the centre of black shade. I sat on a corn shock under a carob tree to eat my lunch of bread and cheese and olives, and it was as cool and refreshing as to sit in water, for the hot runnels of sweat dried on the body without a shiver. As I sat, light as air the body was released of substance and could almost float on the steady breath of wind from the eastern sea. The valley rose terrace on terrace of corn field, red earth, fir trees, grey rock, to a saddle between naked outcrops. Through a gully leading to the saddle lay a mule-track—there was grass on this terrain, grass and flowers and dry, prickly scrub and the pale green gorse plant that sometimes put out spines to grip my ankles, giving me the sensation that the plant had eyes and that it had deliberately clutched me as I passed in order to

draw macabre attention to itself. Overhead, hung large spiders on 'telegraph wire' webs strung with fine engineering and bravado for immense distances, from tree to tree. They shone like steel wires, and to push a way through a really strong web required some force of strength. As I walked the summit-ridge, I met the wind from the eastern sea. One arm of the bay of Limionisa was visible, and at my feet cornfields and a threshing floor, and beyond, a lonely sea. Strong fir trees grew up to the summit on the landward side of this hill named Ere. On the next, lower hill, I saw Agios Profitis Elias, from this eastward side looking quite a different sort of monastery from when I saw it for the first time from the west. I descended through scrub and shale and rock the side of Ere, then up the baking flank of the hill towards the monastery, where once again I found the court-yard deserted and burnished white with sea-wind. As I glided away down the long stone stairs, between the panting, dust-grey sheep, the monk with the killer's hands appeared in the entrance arch, and waved to me. He had perhaps longed to speak with the stranger at the gate, and now with regret, he saw me retreating to the world without having been refreshed with mastika and conversation.

22

Nassuli's father was at the wells, filling his water-tanks, when he started to yell loudly. Varvara and Popi joined in. As he rushed down the steps he began to tear off his leather trouser's belt. Aldo, the boy from across the way, the one who bites, was kicking Nassuli. Aldo escaped into the mountain. Nassuli's father, still swearing, rebuckled his belt.

Two men rowed slowly past, trailing an enormous fish behind the boat, a fish with an ugly head and thick upturned lips and a pinkish body. We were on the ship to Spetsai over the blue-red hissing sea, passing the bleached bones of Ydra, more salt-grey and parch-throated every day, passing Dhokos with its sheer sides and no sign of life at all, just a lighthouse by the water in a pocket of land.

Spetsai was quiet and orderly. We bathed in the fabled waves. A *papas* in grey robes came down to swim. This was life behind glass, muffled and dreamy after the raw emphasis of the other island. Quiet fishermen mended their yellow nylon nets. We sat at the roadside for the sake of getting shade from a tree, and were passed by fiacres and motor cyclists and bronze youths with transistor sets. Everything was relaxed, normal voices, an absence of screams. No donkeys or mules, but quiet horses.

Returning in the evening to the island and the Kala Pigadhia, we were at once hit between the eyes by deafening human cries. Sitting in the salon, I heard commotion under the window. Two donkeys were licking it up the steps, the leader in full bray, mouth open and teeth bared and ears stretched back. The beast was carrying an enormous water storage pot lashed to the saddle. We ran out onto the balcony, under which the man stopped to shout up that the pot was for me. He began to tear at the ropes. I yelled back, no, it was not for me. The man said the *kewpi* had been ordered by an English family with two children. A small crowd had gathered, children came running to join in the fun, screams of panic brought Varvara running. Varvara! We settled into an argument, with extravagant gestures and wild cries of denial, while the women at the wells screamed with delight. The man finished undoing the ropes and as the last one fell from the pot the donkeys moved forward. The un-laden animal trod on the laden one's leading string, bringing him

almost to his knees. We fled into the salon with hands over our ears, expecting to hear the crash of pottery, but the donkey regained its balance, the hoof was freed. The wild man took the pot from the saddle and placed it against the grandmother's house-wall and the old one sat beside it, dumb with surprise. Sophia was away from home. For once, the grandmother would have been glad of the support of her daughter. The man mounted one of the donkeys and slunk off down the steps, keeping close to the wall in the shadow of the cacti, but he did not escape without comment, for Nikos the horseman was riding beautifully up the steps. He shouted at the poor wretch and tapped his head to us to show what he thought of him.

Now that the pot-carrier had gone away, the drama grew less intense, though the washerwoman's daughters still lounged on the steps of the mansion opposite. Beside the wells, the women talked it over.

A black and white goat-kid tripped delicately from the cliffs of Kiapha, to sniff around the pot. One of Sophia's family of mangy cats christened the *kewpi*. At this, the grandmother gave up; one of her own cats had proved it belonged to her cottage, so it must be hers. She raised her hands in a final gesture of defeat, as the cat paced the pot, quivering, tail erect. She sank lower and lower, small and fragile in comparison with the robust jar.

Some time later, the wild man came again, treading softly, and approached the women, who still had not taken home their water-pots. He asked for water to slake his thirst, approached the pot, trundled it to the top of the steps, leant over and somehow hoisted the incubus onto his bowed backbone. He trotted away, like a small beetle with an enormous grain of wheat. By signs, the women indicated to me that he must go back down the Kala Pigadhia as far as the hole for the artificial well, then up whitewashed steps to a house inhabited by a family of English people.

24

Yanis was sitting happily outside a *taverna* in the port, writing on violently pink paper a translation from Greek into French of a love-letter from an Ydriot sailor to a French girl who had been staying on the island. The young man had asked him to embroider it a bit.

'It is best not to be too flowery,' was the scribe's comment.

The sailor had written to her, 'Now that I am back again at sea, I have more time to think of you at night.'

25

'He could only be seen dimly through ochreous dust and green sheets of driven spray, this man. I knew he was searching among the ship-passengers for his woman, who only yesterday went to another island in search of him. In despair that she has not come, he will go away because she is not on any known ship. Never again shall he know the indian moss of her hair, because those who love never meet for more than a short time. It is those for whom we have no passion who shall fill our empty years of Sunday-dinner futility.'

We did no more than bow politely to one another on the few occasions when we met in the port. For all either Leonidas or I cared, this state of affairs could have continued for ever, had not

Yanis suggested that the three of us should dine together one evening, not in the port, but hidden away in a layrinth of streets, a *taverna* with two noble trees in a cobbled courtyard and a table laid for us. There were only workmen, builder's mates, joiners, the old yoghourt vendor, dogs and cats. Dinner consisted of a large fish for each person, salad, and bread. We drank three bottles of retsina, and returned home at midnight, through deserted alleyways.

26

In this time of highest summer a strong youth has become the hornet-slayer, when these insects are thick around the wells. The sound of the rough wooden bat which he uses to destroy them can be heard at first light. When he has succeeded in killing a hornet, he places it carefully in a tin to be used as fishing bait.

The boy comes to the slaughter in the heat of the day. He wears an enormous hat, but his body pays no duty to the sun as he swings and strikes his bat on the cobble-stones.

He returns in the evening for a last assault. Though he kills many beetles, their numbers do not seem to decrease. There is always a new army to buzz around his head, to test the quickness of his wits and arms, the strong young backbone, the whirling legs, the snake-darting head.

Under the shade-tree at the washerwoman's house, one of the daughters is in her slip, wiping the afternoon's sweat away. The old sailor, father of our local seamstress, has just rolled up his trousers at the well, and is washing his legs and feet.

In the mornings, Elene baths on the crumbling platform outside her open door, and after work her husband strips to wash on the

shadowy platform. He is one of the workmen who are drilling the new well-hole half-way down the Kala Pigadhia.

27

Leonidas's house was half-way up the mountain, a sensational climb along broken stone stairways. A portal beneath half-ruined archways within a garden wall, a tangle of jasmine and lemon trees, and succulents. Inside the house a candle-lit kitchen, a black lobster float in the middle of a long table. Up an outside staircase, into a low-ceilinged Turkish room. Above that again, was a music room and a bedroom. The wind was tearing at the house and in the Turkish room, with its platform covered in white rugs and Macedonia carpets in a strong design of Amazons' shields, the air was bitter with smoke from a downdraught.

28

I am the latest person to have been adopted by the hound of Kiapha, a red-coated animal with blue-blind eyes and raw elbows. He lies on the lower patio, moving as the shadows move. He is ghost-silent. Only when I speak to him, does he wag his tail in a resigned salute.

29

Beneath my balcony, Elene's husband was dancing on the flat space between the upper and lower steps, to music from the radio in the grannie's house, while Sophia clapped out the time. He danced with elegance and pride, the fine-drawn Byzantine head poised snake-like on the rigid spine, the legs taut, the feet scarcely moving, long thin feet in spiv's shoes, Saturday evening wear of black and white leather, Greek version of the winkle-picker. He finished the dance by standing on his head for sheer energy's sake. A white cigarette packet fell from his pocket onto the steps. He leapt up and ran across to the grandmother's cottage, and whirled the old woman round the room. She grumbled, pretending to be angry at these attentions, but even though she is eighty, she must still remember the days of her wild pride, and be moved by memory.

30

Perhaps it has to do with the expectation of earthquake that so much latent violence is in the air. There is hot ass-braying, and the brain-drilling of cicadas, and when the rattan curtain on the wall shakes in the hot night-wind, my heart tells me the earthquake is about to destroy us.

For weeks now, we have been expecting the ground to open, for our lives to be endangered.

At last Leonidas, who is more sensitive than the rest of us, for one whole day could not be still but like a wild stallion wandered up and down with dilated eyes in expectation of the shock, which perhaps may have taken place far below the crust of our island or in another country.

Roaring of the black night-sea. The moon, diseased. The sky, red. Thunder and lightning. Suffocating heat, a sense of danger. Wraith-white sailors. Night-strolling crowds. Fire. Earthquake.

31

'There was a one-day strike of ship's crews on the passenger boats running daily to the island from the Piraeus and so in the morning, before the Navy stepped in and broke the strike by sending a pocket battleship filled with islanders, the *agora* was deserted, being reduced to an intimate place without strangers. A half-gale was blowing. The sea leapt at the harbour. Awnings cracked like manœuvred sails.

She walked in the hot red wind, the sun burning her body through a cotton dress of purple, red and dun-green stripes.

He walked in an off-white suit reminding himself of Maupassant and of Tennessee Williams.

She walked with downcast eyes, conscious that he was coming towards her, pretending not to see him.

Larger than life, in their hearts, they swaggered towards one another, he pursuing, she evading, but keeping him well in sight lest at the ultimate moment he should after all be repulsed and pass her by.'

32

Isn't life sad and strange? Some women have ten children and don't really want any of them, and I wanted six sons, but had no children at all.

33

I am too dedicated to life as it goes on in the world, to tempt myself into thinking I could make a nun of me.

How could I ever cut myself off from the simple things of the earth?

This evening, three small girls came to sit on my outer doorstep. Popi was there, nursing a lividly pink doll, and her friend Nela of the lively eyes, and another child whose name escaped me, wearing golden earrings. A small boy joined us. He was carrying a strange plaything or weapon made of bent twigs and leather and blue beads against the evil eye, almost a catapult except that it did not look lethal but decorative. The girls, suddenly becoming spiteful, turned on him laughing and mocking, so that the poor boy, completely discomfited, ran away up the white steps, shamed and distressed by the girls' show of treachery, and at being ridiculed before me, the foreigner.

34

Leonidas was unaware that I was sitting at a table not far away from him at the celebrations on Saturday night, to commemorate the Great Rising against the Turks.

This island bred sea-robbers. In the days when the seas were given over to piracy, her ships were armed against pirates of the Barbary coast. When the time came to rise against the Turkish yoke, the captains of Ydra left their tall stone mansions and sailed up the Aegean with a complete navy financed from their own coffers.

The battery cannons had been firing intermittently throughout the day. At nightfall, there was national dancing on the Agora. When it was quite dark there appeared on top of the mountain the date 1821 made of flambeaux fixed to wooden stakes. A procession of boys carrying flaming torches began to move along the cliff edge above the Battery. They wound towards the town along the rock, appearing dramatically from behind the naval school. They walked the length of the port while the people stood at attention. Cannon roared, fireworks shot across the sky, a boat was burnt beyond the harbour wall as a symbol of the destruction of the Turks, while small craft crossed and recrossed the mouth of the flame-lit port.

The town electricity was turned off, candles were stuck in glasses on the tables outside the cafés.

35

It was a secret joke, never spoken of, that sometime I would write my autobiography, but it should be invented. The opening sentence had been in my mind for years,
'I come of a long line of ladies' maids.'
No, a better construction would be,
'Coming as I do from a long line of ladies' maids it is not surprising that . . .'
What a marvellous springboard into a fictional life.

36

Aldo was discovered to have played truant, and was pursued half-heartedly up the valley. When at last he slunk back, he was caught by the clutching hands of old women, and handed over to his mother. She hit and hit him, while he bellowed and bit at her. Then, at the end of a birch-rod and the tip of her tongue, she drove him up the white steps to the school on the mountain. Many women took part in this drama and were enlivened by it. The boy himself seemed to gain a sort of pride, for the misdeed had coloured the day for him with importance and terror.

37

The crowded port, full of transient foreigners, frightens me at night, but Varvara coaxed me to go down there, and I found myself against my will among the jostling crowd. Yanis was suddenly before us, and it was a surprise, for he looked unnaturally serious. Yanis began talking, in what was plainly a serious mood, with Varvara. I could not understand what he was saying.

Abruptly, he turned to me,

'May I speak alone with you for a minute?'

We walked in the direction of Katsikas, and the post office.

'What is it? What has happened?'

'Leonidas. It happened this afternoon. He has killed a man by accident.'

'I don't believe you. Where did it happen?'

'An Englishman with a big dog, an airedale, was sitting at a table in the port. In passing, Leonidas tripped over the animal. You know how he walks with his head in the air. You know how nervous he is, how violent in his reactions. He flashed out sharply, shouting something about the dog, and the young Englishman leapt to his feet and struck Leonidas in the face. They began to fight, Leonidas pressing the other man towards the water's edge. Having his back to the harbour, the Englishman did not realize how close he was to the kerb of the paving. In fending a blow to his body by Leonidas, he tripped over backwards and fell on the gunwale of one of the moored boats. He died soon after he was taken out of the water.'

'Where is Leonidas? What has happened to him?'

'The police took him away at once, by this evening's ship. He will be imprisoned in the Piraeus.'

'I cannot believe it.'

He has been set apart like a god, by violence.

Time itself has been changed, before and after this disaster. The light-hearted weeks of holiday before this event have been set back into a sharp idyllic distance, so that what I did only yesterday has become something experienced 'five years ago.'

Somehow, reality must be fitted into the dream, the legend with which childhood was filled has to take into itself the present which is the growth of history.

How wounding reality can be, how raw, ever-changing in its patterns, repeating itself under a too-bright sun, sometimes exciting, at other times boring in its repetitions.

I knew at once, the moment I was told of the fight and the mis-adventure, that I could be of assistance to Leonidas; with absolute certainty, that I could perhaps be the only person on the island who was prepared to stand by him.

In retrospect, how sweet were those summer days when, without care, we met casually and exchanged greetings, and passed on, in-different to one another and to fate. How gay I felt under my French straw hat with the purple velvet ribbons.

Going back down the years to childhood, a Leghorn hat with arti-ficial grasses, small silk poppies, cornflowers made of a rough material as decoration, was perfect to me beyond other hats. The word Leghorn was magic in another way, for I had a pet hen of that breed with whom I spent brooding hours crouched in the fork of an undersized apple tree.

It is so much of a relief to put down even a page of words each day, it eases a little the trembling of my hands. I have always been pulled many ways at once, pity has had too great a call on me, but here in Greece I have found the strength to stand hard-fast to a de-cision. How far can I bend before I break, how much salt water cover my head before I drown?

In every year of a life there should be quiet passages where nothing much happens. Now, at this moment, I want to escape the limits of this harsh rock, to be on a kaïki for ten days or so, to know a period of some calm weather, sometimes a short, plunging sea—not idle, it would have been good to help with the painting of ironwork and the cleaning of decks.

The strain of standing by, of being unable to act, and the sense of being watched by unfriendly eyes, is what I find hard to bear.

Can one's experience of life deepen and deepen, or is there a point at which the heart has had too much strain put on it, and surfeited shuts its valves, being unable to expand any more?

This horror had to take place, so that we should be made to struggle towards a rebirth, and painfully learn once more to see and to walk, to begin a new understanding of everything around us in order to forget the old skins we sloughed yesterday.

The measure of strength I have does, I suppose, come to me from the sea. What life would have degenerated into at this period is unimaginable had not the indigo waves run outside my window. It is impossible to stay quietly in the house. The sunshine and movement of wind call bravely from out there, in the sane realism. Their robes flapping in the wind, two of my friends, nuns of Efpraxia, greet me

on the stony whiteness of the road, holding me by the arms. I am clinging to, seeking out, in whatever form it may take, a normal goodness—a new baby being carried in the sun for the first time, the fishermen dancing at Loulou's *taverna* with Yanis, wine-barrels on the edge of the *agora*, more and more of them being placed there to be hosed out, their hoops newly painted, ready for the grape-must which will soon arrive from over the sea, for the new season's retsina. This I am setting against the insane pressures that beset us, the nightmare which shows no sign of ending.

38

Leonidas returned to the island this morning, having been let out on bail pending trial. Grey-faced and tense, he was standing alone in the bow of the white ship. He could have been naked, so vulnerable appeared his face. With staring eyes and puckered mouth, he stretched out his neck for a first view of a friend at the quayside. His shirt was dirty and crumpled, he explained that it had been borrowed from a fellow-prisoner in the jail-house. He, accustomed to appear each day on the waterfront as a handsome hero, had now a tarnished look, a kind of grey stubble seemed to have grown all over him like moss.

I went walking in the upper town among broken steps, seeking out flat pools of shade, trying to quieten my astonished nerves after the relief and strain of his homecoming, needing a little time in which to become calm again before meeting him for lunch in the courtyard with the two trees, the navel of the island. Between one shadow and the next, it came to me, that since I can do nothing practical for him, I must go the harder way, find out what withdrawal and prayer can do. I shall make a temporary withdrawal from the world as long as he is imprisoned by a trick of the gods. The nuns will protect me in the same way as his fellow-prisoners, the safe-breaker, the murderer, will, I imagine, look after him. Before all this happened, Leonidas had encouraged me to go ahead in my desire to seek retreat with the nuns of Efpraxia. Without his support, I would never have gone so far as to ask permission of the mother superior.

Through the perfume of wood-smoke and incense, over the shoe-polished paving stones, in the shadow cast from the house-wall, came the voice: Have patience, everything will happen as it is to happen. Walk quietly in the rhythm of the sea-wind and of the sun, look at the shimmering trees above the goat-well, consider the rocks.

An old woman ran out of her house-door, carrying a flat piece of stone on which incense was burning. She took me into a chapel where she held up a picture of the Virgin, whose tear-filled eyes I kissed.

39

The walled-up wasp holes are still firmly cemented. To Agios Efpraxia, where I asked for and was granted permission to stay as a guest for three days. The nun with whom I always speak told me of how she does not feel the heat, because she has spent most of her life in Egypt.

She said, 'Come up with a little valise. You do not need many clothes in this weather.'

When I asked her how she bore with her black robes, she showed me, they were not after all so heavy.

PART TWO

O SAILORS, O VOYAGERS

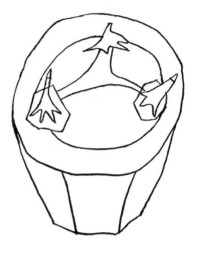

I

THIS cell seems a far cry from the frieze of goats, chocolate-brown, white, flesh-pink animals of race, that range the wooded slopes below. I encountered them on my way up here early this morning in a suddenly archaic Greece of nanny-goats, billy-goats, and kids. The flock-father, old and huge and prehistoric, looked like an invented animal from a bestiary. A woman was drawing water for them at the ruined house where Sibathis had seen his ghost. She was in a white headcloth under a wide hat, the cloth drawn tight across her lower face.

It is early evening. The bespectacled young nun has just returned from her day's shopping in the port. She came through the gate,

wearing a cartwheel straw hat over her black head-covering, and brought her mule to stand at the bottom of the steps within the wall, by the fourth cypress tree, while the other nuns gathered round her to help with unloading the animal, which was afterwards led away to the farmyard by the motherly *mitera* who tends the fowl.

It is a grey evening, as was yesterday's, and so, because there is no glare in the courtyard, the women sit about at the edge of the steps or outside their doors. One is sewing, another is busy with her distaff. It is peaceful, a place in which to write a poem. Here at last I am, for the space of a few days, to live in the highest circle of heaven.

I shall not easily forget my arrival, being taken to a cell, and feeling the inrush of air when the corridor windows and that of the cell were thrown open, and it was possible for me to lean out into the singing air towards the lower mountain ridges, the sea, and the islands.

There is a long, narrow, scrubbed-clean wooden corridor, and opposite each cell's blue door is a large window giving onto the plunging landscape and grey gulf and mysterious islands lying dream-tranced in the midsummer barrenness. It is infinitely quiet, one would scarcely know anyone else inhabited the corridor. When the rising-bell goes at four-fifteen in the morning, there is only a mouse-rustle, and a muted sound of water being run into a tin basin.

In the peaceful end of evening the nuns sit either in a group round the mother superior, or separately, one with spindle and distaff, another wool-carding, drawing out the raw tufts from a sack. In the twisted trees under the terrace, the hens are putting themselves to bed in the highest branches.

Over the reek of fish cooked on charcoal was suddenly swung the smell of incense from a brazen dish, a nun casting the fragrance out onto the terrace, across the fish-fumes.

After vespers, in a hazy moonshine, the lame nun brought my supper, fish and tomato salad, bread, and a carafe of water.

A nun came to tell me the electric dynamo was going to be turned off, and to see that I had a bees' wax taper and matches.

When I was already in bed, another nun, the friendly one who often sighs, came in with a glass of water skinned with oil onto which she flaked pieces of candle-fat around a metal and cork object. This she placed in my wall-cupboard. I examined the glass after she had gone. On the film of oil covering the water floated the metal and corks. On each piece of cork was impaled a petal from a white mountain flower. Twisted thread formed the wick of this primitive night-light, and it was threaded through the tin and cork and petal, to be lit at the end of the sepal. Moths and flies floated on the surface of the oil.

2

The Orthodox day begins at a quarter past four in the morning. At Efpraxia, the bell is rung urgently, there is a rustle, a pause, then the bee-humming of prayer begins in the chapel, to go on until about a quarter to eight.

My breakfast is brought to me by the cheerfully-smiling lame nun: coffee, rusks, sheeps' milk with sugar, and a glass of water.

The midday meal is sparse, but as today is Sunday, there is *arni psito*, lamb on the knucklebone, strong goat-cheese, macaroni, cheese and tomato sauce, water melon for dessert.

After the first evening, when I was obsessively hungry, I have felt quite satisfied even though I have been working and walking every day. At half-past four in the afternoon I am brought a cup of Turkish coffee, a glass of cold water, and rusks. After evensong in the chapel, I take my tray of supper to my cell. Following this meal, there is another, chanted service which in such hot weather is conducted outside under the vine-trellis.

Three tired nuns standing in the lower courtyard leant their weary arms on the higher level, giggling at the antics of a cat leaping after insects and moths. This cat is an expert catcher of cicadas, and will flush one out of the trees near the wall, pursue it over the courtyard, even so far as to end the hunt in the mother superior's room.

Tonight being full moon, the dynamo was not turned on, and the service was conducted under brightness spreading from the eastern sky.

The night was so clear I could not sleep. For a long time I looked from my window at the hard clarity of the courtyard and the chapel and the sharp cypresses unstirred by wind.

There is no sense of constraint here. All is cheerful busyness, with spells for rest and gossip. It is a hard life which shows itself plainly in the faces of the nuns. They do not have enough sleep—about six hours a night, and one or two hours for siesta. The youngest nun has charge of the mules, and she rides down every day to Ydra on shopping excursions, from which she returns with loads of timber and mattresses and food. On some days she does not return until dusk, having been down in the port for the whole day, and while the others are at service in the chapel she has to water and feed the mules, and anoint their saddle-sores.

High on this mountain-top, I can at last sleep again. At the Kala Pigadhia, I had entirely lost my sleep, because of the many night-disturbances, and the oppression of heat.

Here I have come to be out of the world for a spell, wishing to put to the test whether I am in greater need of the world or of the non-world, and to pray for Leonidas.

3

At dawn, a miraculous rain was falling freshly on the parched earth. I dozed in and out of chanting from the chapel, mixed with a strong dream of being menaced by a bull. Soon the harsh, flat tones of the holy mothers were joined by the deep voice of the old *papas* from Profitis Elias. At about seven o'clock, the *papas* went back to his own monastery, but first he stopped to talk to the flowers and a tree inside the gateway.

As he went slowly up among the rocks, his stick tap-tapping on the way, he was joined by the farmer and four belled mules which were being brought back from the grazing ground of the lower mountain

slopes to begin their morning's work at the threshing floor.

The primitive nun who had cooked last night's supper of fish and who came out to the chapel rolling her sleeves down over greasy arms, saying in effect 'It's ready when you are,' brought me my breakfast. She is so intrigued by me that she does everyting in slow motion around me in order to have time for study. She proffered the tray with infinite slowness; coffee and rusks and water, then she came back to fill my water carafe. She still watched me open-mouthed as she went down the stair-ladder, keeping her eyes level with the floor, gloating over me until the last moment.

My Yemenite ring fascinates and amuses the nuns, and the old one at the end of the corridor stopped dead when she saw me in a black silk petticoat with black lace edging. I wear black underwear, the nuns favour violet.

Leonidas who is on bail pending his trial, had said he would bring breakfast on this first morning up the mountain. On the red earth track towards the long steps, I came face to face with him. He said, 'Hello, you have not changed.' He had brought black cherries, hard-boiled eggs, and a thermos of iced Demestika wine.

Here then, as we clinked glasses, was the moment when my battle-camps were placed side by side, the worldly and the spiritual, but because it was on Greek soil there was no real conflict, for who could raise so much as a faint warcry in this daylight where to live one must seek a shadow only to find that a shadow is full of light, and that both light and shade are drowned in the thunder of cicadas in an elemental morning that sees hundreds of goats on the move? Tomorrow they will have been forgotten on these same slopes, in a morning freshened by the piled-up thunderheads having been dissipated and purged by the shower that fell in the dark time of the night, rain so unusual it took me in one step, my cell being small, to the window where I could feel the trees' and flowers' deep satisfaction, for as one of the nuns had told me, 'July finds it difficult to rain.'

(White tents were raised up, facing one another. Pennants ran out along the wind. Soldiers lolled on the burnt earth under the shade-trees. Idly, the enemy forces looked at one another. Forgetting the cause for which they were fighting, they stared into one another's eyes.)

Did Leonidas climb so far and so high just to help keep me in the world? He said, 'You must see Patmos. I could have lived on Patmos.' I wondered yet again why he is always so nervous, so irritably eager to get away as soon as he has reached a destination. He is a man on the run, he thinks it is from others he wishes to escape, but it is really himself from whom he wants to hide.

Pursued by his devils, he rushed away down the long steps, towards the mountain-track and the safety of the port, and I went in the opposite direction, towards the monastery of Holy Elias.

The strap of one of my sandals broke. It was impossible to walk any further in it, so I sat down on a step and waited for help to come out of the air.

A workman I knew already from having seen him passing by the wells, came out of the main door of the monastery, with a whitewash brush in his hand. With a piece of fine wire he bound the broken strap, and he patted me in friendly fashion on the back when he understood I was a guest of the nuns. The small son of the shepherd at the monastery sat beside us with a goat-kid which he dragged towards me for my admiration.

4

Mist hung around the mountain-top and a chill penetrated into the weaving room where three nuns were working. Two were weaving, and the simple-minded Wrinkle-face was wool-carding in a corner, muttering and laughing to herself. From time to time she approached

the weaving-frames and put out a hand to touch the threads, but each time she was ordered to return to her own work.

In the middle of the morning, Rosy Pie-face went out for a few moments, and returned with the present of an apple for me. A clammy coldness grew over me as I sat in the sunless room, but I was afraid to leave for fear of hurting the feelings of the women.

We found an old peasant seated in the outer kitchen when we came up from the work-shed. She told me she was sick and very poor, and produced a few coins from a carefully folded handkerchief, saying it was all the money she had. Beside her was a bundle and a stick. We were each given a meal in separate cells, a meal of potatoes and egg-plant stuffed with rice.

The canary-cage was hanging askew on the house-wall.

'Beloved bird, O my poor bird!' cried the Outdoor nun. 'What has the cat done to you?'

She took the bird out of the cage, and spreading one of its wings, disclosed a wound at the side of its breast.

'Bring the iodine quickly,' she cried out to Rosy Pie-face. She dabbed iodine on the bird's side, and spoke lovingly to it before putting the cage on the front wall of the chapel.

The cat, sleek and petted, sat irritably washing its paws. Happy, happy Efpraxia cat, stretched out her hairy length, without a care in the world, little knowing that down in Ydra her life would be scarcely worth living, that she would be ravaged and aged before her time, always hungry, always brawling, kicked by children, chased by dogs, a Thing versus the Rat.

5

A new life has begun for me in the second cell from the east by south end of the building. It is small and fresh and bare, I have everything that is necessary—a sink outside the door, a wall cupboard for keeping articles such as bread saved from meals, nails behind the door for my bags and clothes, a chair, a pallet, a table for my tray of food at mealtimes. On the windowsills in the corridor are small personal belongings, a bar of pale green soap, a water pot, a lavender handkerchief (a surprise: underwear and handerkchiefs are lavender-coloured, almost exotic). The staircase down to the ground-floor is little more than a ladder, and the hall is bees' waxed and mirror-bright. Plants with huge glossy leaves have been trained to grow along the ceiling. There are flowers and potted plants everywhere. In the evening, a singing bird is hung in its cage against the chapel wall. The mother superior frequently goes into the shadowy kitchens to superintend the cooking.

One of the nuns likes to lie on her bed in the morning reading the newspaper. I sometimes hear her washing up dishes at the sink in the corridor, and this afternoon I met her eating a honey cake.

6

A world grey as feathers, cicadas competing with the thunder. A ferocious heat: the slopes of grey rock and whitened herbs in certain places taking the full sun seemed to be lit with thick flames, the air was filled with the smell of scorching, cicadas plopped from the trees, shrieked, cackled, swooped. Dragonflies glistened, grasshoppers, displaying every variation of red and green and yellow under-body, clicked and leapt along my path. Only under the occasional tree was there a breeze and some shade.

It became necessary to seek shelter from so much fire and feverish tumult. I went up to my cell, leaving the door to the corridor open so as to catch as much air as possible. As I lay on the bed, feeling

the subsidence of the shale-flames behind my eyes, the weather gradually darkened towards a thunderstorm. It grew more and more still, and as thunder began to roll along the mainland heights, the cicadas too gave up their noise, clinging unknowably to the pine-tree trunks. The slopes had become almost transparent in their remote whiteness, the sea lay utterly becalmed, thick and pale as milk. O voyagers, O sailors, on the milk-white sea.

7

It is time for a stocktaking of the spirit during this period of being cut off physically from one another, and from the movements of our world.

Are we, because we live in the classical context of Greece, simply puppets hounded and bewildered by the Furies?

I have always been committed to the work of my mind and hands. Now, against all reason, I commit myself to Leonidas. Isn't the secret of living, to be committed to someone, to something? Quite apart from putting trust in God, which of course he does, he desires desperately to put his whole earthly trust in another person, but because of his ambivalent nature, he dare not. He should try and learn to trust. Life goes on a long while for some of us, and there is always the chance of a miracle round the next headland.

A friend, a Benedictine monk, once told me I was a fool to put my trust in anyone but God. This seems a comparatively easy thing to say if one is living out of the world in any sort of monastic community, though Man's senses anywhere are not that easily subdued. All I know is that for me it is necessary to put trust in other people. If I ceased to be able to do that, I'd find it impossible to go on living.

A person can say arrogantly, 'I'm not going to let myself be hurt again,' and can find himself injured. Ultimately we hurt ourselves by punishing other people. In this way, we grow sick inside.

Perhaps Leonidas should have overheard a conversation Yanis and I had at Graphos' a few weeks ago. Had he been there to eavesdrop he would have learned more about me than I ever told him. It is easier to speak to Yanis than to Leonidas about such things because Yanis is outside my emotional life, though I think sympathetic to me.

Doestoyevsky, in one sentence, has condensed what it took many words for me to express that night.

'For a woman, all resurrection, all salvation, from whatever perdition, lies in love; in fact, it is her only way to it.'

I believe human life is only possible if we can be sure that another person or even an animal depends on us. In a prison cell, the bird coaxed through the bars, the mouse or the rat come for crumbs.

Men and women being human to one another partake of the sacrament.

8

I was lying on my back, listening to the murmured prayers from the chapel and thinking of getting up when the children Popi and Nassuli appeared in my line of vision, coming down the steps towards the gate of the *monasteri*. I sprang out of bed and peered from the small window. Fortunately, they went back up the steps onto the little patch of flat ground which brought them level with my window, so that I was able to signal to them that I had seen them and that the nuns were still at prayer. They had to wait about an hour for me. I had tried to go out, but one of the nuns had stopped me because I had not yet had my coffee, and she was shocked that I thought of going out without breakfast.

I was given a cup of goats' milk as well as coffee, which made me feel guilty as this was the second morning on which I had had two breakfasts. Varvara had sent up hard-boiled eggs, bread and butter, and retsina, with a note telling me that Leonidas would soon be called away for trial on the mainland.

We sat under the trees among the old terraces on the slope between Elias and Efpraxia, until it was time for the children to return to their goats which were grazing further down the mountain.

From about twelve-thirty in the afternoon, there was a deep silence of siesta. Suddenly and very clearly, could be heard the sound of a brass-band in Ydra.

Outside the gate the cicadas were deafening.

By half-past three, the voices of the nuns were again to be heard gossiping in the kitchens and living quarters. While I was making a drawing on the terrace, a nun brought me a cup of coffee and rusks.

9

I ventured out under the bronze sky, to follow the high path along the contour of the opposite mountain. The track was rocky and airy, easy-going. Nothing moved there except for two mules and a donkey who passed without interest. The sun menaced me with so godlike a tread that at last I was forced to hide on a flat rock overshadowed by a small juniper. Into this uncomfortable tree I managed to insinuate myself for a siesta, though I could not sleep for thinking of Leonidas.

Returning over the top of the ridge, I came upon the two farmer brothers winnowing corn at Profitis Elias. One man, barefoot, tossed the grain over and over with a wooden paddle in the breeze so ideal for separating grain from husks, while his brother brushed aside the chaff. The breeze carried away the pale golden shower of fine straw.

At Efpraxia, the youngest monk from Elias was coming out of the kitchen. The huge rough man with the killer's hands, scruffy and fierce-seeming, was carrying a hunk of bread wrapped in paper.

Long-drawn out preparations are going forward in readiness for the Saint's Day on July the twenty-fifth. A nun has just come down from Profitis Elias with sweet-smelling waxcandles made by the monks for the feast day. We savoured the smell of them.

At this time of day and because the weather is cloudy, almost all the nuns are in the courtyard.

10

The nuns: perhaps it is their good fortune that they do not know the pangs of love, jealousy, envy of another woman's beauty. I wish it were permissible to ask them how much they endured before they became patient and humble and without thought of themselves.

11

The experience of living in an Orthodox nunnery cuts clean across the dream of classical myth into which I had thought to sink. The old gods are almost if not quite dead.

12

For breakfast, an extra treat: a saucerful of pale gold and brown currants, and nuts sprinkled with sugar and cinnamon. The Hopalong nun was helping herself to them as she came along the corridor to my room.

The Outside nun has just ridden away across the mountain with two mules, one heavily laden with mattresses. The strong wind was blowing her hat about.

13

The community finds me docile and compliant. Me, or the half of me, I'm a gargoyle in a corner of the terrace, leaning out over the world. Two young men are down there in a *taverna* dancing with taut bodies and rigid necks, hissing softly at one another. The nuns do not know of what I am thinking. It is a large comfort to be with people devoid of second sight. Just as they can have no conception of the wildness of my feelings, so they have no jealousy, but treat me as a rare bird flown in from overseas to rest for a few days under the shadow of their vine-stock.

14

If there is any sense of being imprisoned, then it comes out of something born in all of us. To be alive is to be trapped within the flesh, within the mind, within the pattern of days and nights.

It is not only that I am enclosed in this cell, whitewashed, with a hard bed, a small window, but since first I saw light, even before that time, I was cell-enclosed, for no one of us can burst into a real freedom from our case of flesh. I, you, each in a separate cell, a cocoon of self, which we cannot disown or creep from, or break, or exchange for another, must submit to this confinement with what-

G

ever grace lies in us. We are enveloped in flesh, and in that flesh the soul, the mind, and the heart are imprisoned until death.

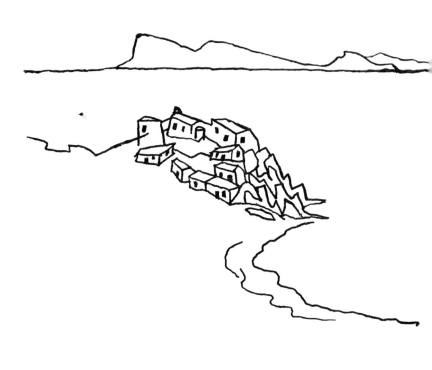

15

In this cell there is nothing to disturb my thoughts. I am free to range backward over the drowthy months. I wonder if Leonidas remembers Sunday night the fourteenth of July?

'Vive la France!' shouted Pan Aristidi, raising his glass over the darkness that was the sea below the cliff-edge. We were at the *taverna* along the coast at Vlichos which Michalis had discovered to us one night when we were passing in his boat. He had played his torch over the small chapel, and the low thatched huts, under the shelter of the mountains. Below the *taverna* is a primitive jetty from which that morning Michalis had given a lift in the boat to a handsome lean man and a plain woman carrying between them a heavy wicker-covered wine-jar.

Beside a church at the cliff-edge, two old people were sitting in the late light. Many small children tumbled in the dust not far away.

The *taverna* is kept by an elderly couple, tall and noble, very much alike in looks and bearing, she like a benignant queen, he with a withdrawn dignity—the couple I had been hoping to see again, since the Sunday of the feast day in Ermioni when I had noticed them waiting on the *agora* for the ship, regal and serenely smiling, with tall wax candles and bags of provisions for the day and night of vigil. And their son was the handsome man of the morning, he of the wine-jar. The old man was dressed in pale blue, baggy-seated trousers in the old style, with large white buttons from waist to flies, a white singlet, and a woollen fringed cummerbund.

We were given unlimited retsina, fish, salad, cheese, and dessert was a water-melon.

16

It being Sunday, the nuns have washed their clothes. They hung their black skirts and tunics to dry under the house-vine. Wide lavender nightgowns, lavender bust-bodices, knickers and hand-kerchiefs.

99

17

This was to be an afternoon of daylight dream. As protection against
the sun, I wore a white head-covering. Among the grasshoppers, the
marching ants, the armoured beetles, I passed through the shade of
the wood by the ruined house where Sibathis had seen his ghost-man.

Steps led up to patches of cultivated ground where vines and fruit
trees grew. Westward, a scarf of heat lay over the islands. Climbing
the last stair, I passed a long farm building, and came out onto an
earth-covered terrace bordered with shade-trees. A mule was walking
across this terrace in search of water.

Over the porch at the gateway to the *monasteri* was a fresco-painting
of Holy Elias, barbaric, fierce-eyed, driving his team of four red-ochre
horses, the sun-god driving his steeds across heaven. One wing of

the door was open into a courtyard dazzled with light. Intense silence of light, light on stones, penetrative light, enfolding, embracing, comforting light pouring out of the rock. It was sensuous and subtle, no harsh beating-down of sun-rays, but a white diffuseness. Light, and an absolute silence, not an absence of sound. The courtyard was empty save for this singing fullness of bright air. The church standing towards the eastern end of the courtyard was brilliantly clear and yet improbable as a dream, each long stone of it outlined with whitewash.

A monk began to chant in one of the cells. I tiptoed about the tranced yard, in fear that someone would come out of a door and destroy my dream.

Through the gateway I looked down onto the other world. On the upper stone stairs framing the waters of the harbour, under dark trees, a flock of sheep lay stretched out panting in the dust. They stirred as I walked amongst them, and the clang of their bells sounded above the chirping of crickets. I looked back at the sun-god driving his horses, at the marble bell-tower rising above the trees. Below lay Ydra with its sea-traffic and its crippled sponge-fishers.

18

I went to where the mother superior and two of the miteras were sitting under the vine.

'The three days are over. It has been a wonderful time. Tomorrow I must return to Ydra.'

They looked at one another, and laughed.

'You are welcome to stay here as long as you like,' said the mother superior.

I relax and am happy in the atmosphere of order and peace created by the good mothers, but for how long could I be content to stay with them? I should soon become rebellious, the haven would become a prison, I'd remember Michalis in his boat at daybreak, of how he ran out his line astern, and how he listened for the nibble of the little fish. I'd find myself in imagination, sitting on the bow under a sun-awning, thinking of Leonidas and of how I wanted to be near him at his trial, and I'd remember how I looked at the mountains barring me from him, not sad or even melancholy, but gay, drinking the sun and the wind, filled with water-dazzle and companionship, ready to come home and do battle with him for the right to be at his side, but also ready to give in if he refused to have me there; and I was suddenly wide awake, present in the boat, and watchful of the men, Michalis and his friend, how they in different ways despatched their fish. The old man (one would have thought he was handling a tunny) killed his catch by hurling each tiny body to the deck. Michalis did it by biting the head of the fish in his strong white teeth.

20

There need only be a glimpse of salt water, a *kaïki*, a wind-shaken flag, a swaying mast, and I am myself again, a translated being under dark or white sail—and overboard to the oyster, octopus, and squid, go my reverse-aspiring thoughts. It was not cowardice brought me up the mountain. It was that I did hope to gain knowledge of the Spirit, and thought to have learned, if only a little, and yet—now, one spray shot through with fire convulses me. Could I ever be enchained to a still life of patience and security? Never. I am for ocean, the tumult of *thalassa*, bluer than midnight, for black-skinned seamen bearing baskets of coral, bearded oysters, and fish stranger than my friends.

From this terrace-eyrie of the interior, I have only to look down and under my hand, my eyes, my heart, is Leonidas's empty house, just distinguishable from the other clustered cubes. There is white jasmine and white pillars against the tawny mountain above the cemetery. Leonidas's ghost is watering plants in the early evening that will not cool with nightfall, but will burn into the early hours

of Monday, with cockcrow telling every hour, cats screaming at the door, a red warning light at the end of the harbour. His ghost is wearing a dark shirt, and his feet are bare and long under the pale trousers I patched for him.

I wish I could stop the trembling of my hands. How one sweats and sweats.

Thinking back to everything that happened 'five years ago' and 'Do you remember, how we joined the wedding party near Kaminia, and how the bride threw gauzy packages of sweets down to our boat from an upstairs window?' my heart stands at the memory of it, for it has been overlaid by so many shadows, sometimes I despair of seeing through them again to the light.

With blaring of horns, with shouts and laughter, our boat swept to the jetty, and one wedding-guest, then another, leapt onto our benzina with trays of drinks and highly-spiced meat-balls. And later, while we were dining, the wedding-guests had swept under the cliff in two boat-loads. In the early hours of the morning we drifted out towards the Peloponnesos, and slowly back again until we were under the island, trailing our hands in the phosphorescent sea, and talking under the influence of the stars.

22

Looking down onto the port, I see the racing donkey-boys, I hear the siren of the ship that daily brings adventurers and letters, adventurers, a few letters, many adventuresses hawking their ancient trade about the Aegean. The harbour waits to absorb the women, and cynical men wait to seduce them, to pick them up where they sunbathe on the cement rocks.

Looking down onto the port, I see Captain Theophanis, the vision of God. He has whale-bone shoulders, a suffering smile, and a corseted waist. The smell of salt water embarrasses him; the waves lapping so quietly at the port, even they cause him to think uneasily of the phantom liners whose bridges he has never paced during thick nights on the Atlantic run.

'And what of Java, Captain? Knowest thou Sumatra?' What becomes of him in winter-time when the orange lights have been put out in the restaurant, when the orange hammocks have been taken in, when the doors are padlocked?

To a *kafeneion* in the Piraeus did he but last night return from a journey up the Amazon, only to find his landlegs rusted and unreliable?

It is possible to live a lie until it is a kind of truth, until a beauty comes out of even so timid a pretence.

Captain Theophanis, I salute you among the painted caiques.

23

A night of uttermost beauty and calm, poignant with loss and painful memories. Dreaming islands, lighted ships, the Saturday night *agora* mercifully remote. As the dawn came, I slipped along the corridor and down the ladder onto the terrace beyond the public kitchen, to see the first light come over Ydra. The idyllic mood of weather, and the background of the peaceful *monasteri*, was unberable.

On the white espalier, a vine.

Youths and maidens, two by two, trot and canter their donkeys along the sea-road towards Mandraki. The red dust road, the emerald sea with deep-lying rocks clear in it, lie in the path of the mainland that every day grows more defined and like a lived-in landscape of real houses, farms, lemon groves, battlefields, shores, beaches for the drawing-up of boats, men, children, women, mules. A landscape that I remember. The Hopalong nun limped out from the cistern-house on to the lower patio, carrying a cloth and a pail of water, with which to sponge down the leaves of a plant speckled with red rain from the desert.

24

Sometimes, truly, it would appear that life as it is called, is part of the world of dreams.

It was on the Athens-Patras road a year ago, where we explored a small road leading into the mountains, the point at which I should have simply vanished into another sort of existence. It is a dirt road running between the sand-coloured soil of the olive groves. We encountered peasants with their goats going up into a village hidden in trees. The goats, startled by our approach, ran among the ancient olive-stems. I think I should have gone with those people, and helped to look after their flock, the magnet being that the sea was only down the road, and the wild stones began where the village ended. It would have been the best of both my worlds: fishes, air-bleached caiques, flowers, aggressive wide-trumpeted lilies, olive and lemon groves, and naked mountains of the Peloponnese.

Was it a real ferry-boat on which we crossed the Gulf of Patras? Was it the crossing of the Styx? The opposite shore was full of terror, but Metéora drew us more strongly than fear kept us on the sea-road. A ruined battery or castle was beside the ferry, the sea was like no known sea, boiling with green light, offering death. Within the boiling of the Gulf, were two ships, one sideways to the northern shore, one dreamily making for our side. The wind, more violent with each fearful breath we drew, flung sprays into the afternoon rain. The ferry-boat came at the shore, the car-ramp was lowered, ropes were secured to the land. Passengers and lorries and buses came off. A tall priest struggled with his robes. His hat, desired by the wind, he clutched. With fine shivering, experienced fear, we went aboard and felt the tension of the crew, the manœuvring of the ship from its berth, the turning, twisting revolutions. Sense of direction left us. Rain-blinded windows, the shore going away, sea-seeth becoming greater. Haunted ferry-boat!

A gipsy stood up and blew upon a long pipe, and I looked for the cobra and the basket, but there was no snake. He was fear-charming us not to look through the raining window.

What! The same shore, the same battery or castle. We had not left the Patras side at all, but gone full circle. The always feared, never-before experienced *back to where we started from*.

Desperately, we ran out of the ship, but *orientation we made come*; inventing mountains, inventing the north, to find reassurance in a toy harbour, but there again—a dream-kaïki, of too-perfect shape to have conviction lay anchored in the shelter of the sea-wall.

And the sea smote the land. Lightning and thunder. Rain. None of it was real.

A headache-punctuated ride through mountains awash with torrents and stone. Rock, and ear-numbing altitude.

Was Walrus-whiskers who sang *bazouki* songs in the *taverna* at Lidoviki, was he real? Why, if not flesh, did I dream him?

We tried to escape from the rain and the still memory of the haunted ferry-boat and the gipsy singer, by eating a dinner of fish and by drinking a retsina whose flavour we could not recognize. This was a Wednesday, of no significance.

Leonidas is real because he owns a dog, and the dog is in the port, and I can walk beside the dog, and can think logically, 'If the animal exists that is owned by a certain man now absent, then it follows that the man exists in order to have brought the dog to this particular island.'

That night with no cessation of the rain, we slept under a tree with a gigantic bole, and thunder shook its roots.

The dream continued. Women passed in the first light, riding-queens moving towards the valley where first I scented wolves, and the squalor of stinking privies, carcases, and wet hides. Dogs prowled the morning puddles, and the river-beds were yellow as lions.

The gipsy encampment was not in my delirium. The river-bed in which the Transylvanians had made their home was suddenly filled with flood-water. On our bank of the river, tents and children; on the seaward side, tents, women and horses. Women in their familiar blankets cried out across the turbulence,

'Who will save us from the rising of the waters?'

They existed, we were not in their dream, but they were in ours. The black-haired, long-plaited heads of the women with their blankets, horses, children and tents, brought deep trouble into our dream.

Around Amphissa, the cart-horses had no bits or bridles, only rope halters around their faces. The women, with mysterious hair drawn low across the brow, wore traditional costume, a long-skirted sleeveless coat over blouse and skirt and apron.

A land of horses, turkeys, sheep, shepherds in hooded cloaks. Dead dogs on the road. Tents, cottages necklaced with Indian corn.

Ever northwards pressed we danger back on a diet of bread and cheese, olives, apples, and hope.

Seabed-discovered Metéora reared above us, cloud-maddened pillars, evil shapes built of sea-pebbles. A phallus. Gashes, gaping mouths, the drained ocean-bottom become habitable. How strange that these rocks, the ultimate in evil, should have been taken over for the service of God, perhaps to fight the Devil on his uttermost territory. Platforms, chains, baskets, space between the floorboards. These men pushed solitude to its furthest point, but did they not, like Seraphim, spend much time looking out of the window for the chance traveller? It is the hermit talks most when he can find a wedding-guest, for speech is natural to us, and, unnaturally kept down, bursts out in talk to the snail and the flower and the cat.

And what of Seraphim, who saw us coming a long way off, and who had the ouzo out and ready and had himself taken a thimbleful for relief that someone cared enough to climb to his monastery in the air. The visitors' book was ready, and the begging bowl, and the long tale of wrongs done to him. Most fantastical, the double-beds of shining brass in clean bedrooms waiting for guests who would never come, for it is necessary to bring your own food here. Seraphim has nothing to offer except ouzo and conversation and a leaky roof and a floor with holes onto space and frescoes with bullet-holes in them, and an absence of chalices, vestments or jewelled maces or illuminated manuscripts, and fierce coldness in winter-time and cruel burning of summer heat. O, he will tell you the names of every snail on the path, the names of the monk-skulls and flowers. He talks with stones and God, and when there is a market-day in the village below, he goes down in the evening to the mud and the disorder and the coloured rugs, brown, dark-red, that the peasants throw over themselves as protection against the rain while they are selling their wares, stone pots and jars, and vegetables and fruit. They pile the sodden rugs head-high, and will not sell them. I saw a child on a cart before his father's body, protected by the father's arm and a coloured rug.

If a real ferry-boat crosses the Gulf of Patras, then Seraphim is flesh and bone. He talks of Communist vandals, and of the nuns who have taken over the further *monasteri*, the one in which he was quite happy to be alone, but here, he is too aware of the hangman's drop under the floor. The Virgin in the chapel reminds him of what is soon to come, his own laying-out he can experience over and over again in the shed of skulls.

I tell you again, the mountain road we were hoping to take near Patras had been washed away, so one of us said, 'Let's go to Metéora.'

We went, and came alive out of those mountains. The rain never ceased, thunder and lightning went on and on, the road was a river-bed in places, and it felt as though the mountain-range would fall on us. We were expected. Everywhere we went, we were expected.

We went far north, towards the Pindus.

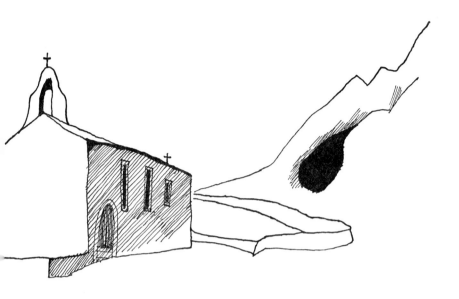

At Metéora, a wolf barked at night. We heard it through the wind and rain as we cowered in our bags at night. In the morning, birds sang, their voices amplified, in the mouth-shaped niches of the monoliths.

Hermit-caves, platforms, chains. Seraphim was so pleased to see us, 85 years old, and talking to the snails, telling them to come out and eat, to enjoy themselves.

He smiled, saying, 'Soon, it will be my turn to be placed there. Come out, little snail, and eat.'

There was a brown grease-woman in Lamia, a woman made to be pinched, and she was cooking camel meat, and in between times was with a pole unhitching sausages from the ceiling, and I was the whole time sinking lower onto the table from the smell of ZOO. Under a trapdoor her husband descended among the camel-carcases, and was unabashed. For him, it was the scent of home.

A gipsy-boy stood beside a cross-eyed Turk type, opened his voice, and his whole frame quivered with the passionless passion of his

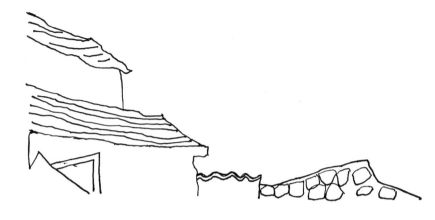

song. The Turk-type desired him. We gave him money and fish. His face was beautiful, without expression. He had no thoughts. The Turk-type's eyes were more cross-grained than ever, as he listened to the throbbing notes from the boy's throat.

Through mountains then, in dangerous darkness. After the high lands, we came to a fertile plain of tents, and embroidered women, a ruined mosque sprouting a living tree, a pool of water, a shop smelling of new bread and incense and black braids of hair, wet under handkerchiefs edged with sequins.

He liked me, that unspeakably dirty old monk in the northern mountains. His clothes stank of grease and charcoal smoke. The palms of his hands were black-ingrained. He had blackened teeth too, but there was something jolly, a living gaiety, about him, when we met in the rain on that lost road towards the Pindus. He was standing under a tree, waiting for a christening party to come down from the region of the high dam. We were sheltering in the church when they came in, the *papas* and the women and children with a basket of food for the feast afterwards. The women prostrated themselves before the *eikonostasion* in prayer, the child to be baptized having first been laid on a blanket beneath an ikon.

It came to Sunday, when we broke our fast with cinnamon-flavoured milk.

Why should we, on our return towards the Argosaronikos, have stepped aside to visit this other island, Évia, if not to witness the pelican being harried out of the sea? A Sunday morning mob pressed down the steps almost into the water from which the persecuted fish-eater struggled with awkward feet and slowly-flapping wings. Forced out of the harbour, the pendulous bird was lost in the crowd that surged into the town, and was borne along, hemmed in midst of craven persecution towards the police-station, a bloody-breasted bird, to be accused of what? Of simply being the axe-beaked pelican, the self-wounder destined to be mob-wounded. This bird had been tried and found guilty by the people of Chalkis long before it had reached the law courts.

What sore place in my consciousness is touched by the memory of the pious bird? Leonidas on the waterfront at Ydra! The bird has taught me what the man suffered when he was taken by the people.

25

The only thing I want to do is to sleep and sleep for hours, days, nights, weeks, to shed the strain of the past months. I am beyond weeping, beyond emotion. I only want to sleep. And do, without effort, without dreams.

The last dream I can remember having had was the 'total withdrawal' or 'death' dream in Athens, in the middle of the afternoon, the effect of which was so strong that it convinced me that Leonidas was dead or would not be there to meet me at the café at seven-thirty, as he had said he would be, at the junction of Ermou and Plateia

Syntagma. He had appeared to telephone me. I knew it was his voice, though he was scarcely audible. I knew he was deliberately muffling his voice in order to confuse me, by implication to show that he was going out of my life, without reason. And the next day, even after he had been there, I began to wonder if I had dreamed his presence, as I had dreamed his withdrawal.

That is what life is, too. Violent encounters, inexplicable withdrawals.

26

We have to learn to overcome the fear of growing old, of the years that press us down towards the grave, or we shall be paralysed into inaction.

One of the agonies of mankind is to be impatient, to be unable to accept the natural speed of life, to want time here compressed, there extended out of season.

Time stand still. Time pass! Learning to live with oneself is mortally hard. Who is this woman I stare at in the mirror? Did I invent her, or did she make me up in the glass?

And Leonidas, have I invented him too, because he was necessary to me? No, he is a real man in a world he calls dismal, and he is real to me because he is afraid and has begun to conquer his fear.

I suddenly felt it was imperative that I should return to the port before it was too difficult to go back into the world, so I cleaned out my cell and packed my goat-hair bag. I told the mother superior of my intention of leaving before the day grew too oppressive, but she persuaded me to stay until the late afternoon.

'They are making something especially good for lunch today,' she said, 'and there will be time for a siesta before you go down the mountain.'

My knees began to tremble as soon as I got out of sight of the monasteri, and I found myself walking more and more slowly towards the houses and the sound of voices. A praying mantis, going in the opposite direction, stopped when it saw me, and turned back for another look. I crouched down, the mantis reared upright for a closer inspection, before resuming its journey.

PART THREE

THIS ISLAND BURNS ME

I

IT is as if I had been away from the port not for days but for years. Uncertain what to say to the people I know, I felt it imperative to seek them out at once, to get over as soon as possible my sense of strangeness.

Leonidas, a harried ghost, flits from his house to the post office and back, hoping for news from his legal advisers in Athens. His nerves have brought him to the edge of breakdown.

I tell myself, search not your soul, lest you find a particularly hairy spider in one of the corners.

Every scrap of self-pity I ever had has been burned away by the sun, washed out of me by the warm sea. If you pity yourself here, then you are truly to be pitied. Seek not to search my soul, lest you find it contain a hairier and more long-legged spider than you bargain for. You do not want my spider to devour yours, do you now?

Every sound, every sight in the smallness of an island is an invocation, an incantation. The run of green water across the harbour-mouth when the wind is from the north, the striking of eleven o'clock from the campanile in town, eleven o'clock, and the mail-boat hooting as she breasts around the mole!

The reverberations of noon, struck too forcibly from the bell in the echoing tower.

Mandarin oranges on a leafy branch, gifted by a full moon among the rocks.

The moon heels westward over Greece.

2

Two young men were swimming in heavy weather. They found it impossible to get out of the water because of the raggedness of the rocks and the presence of sea-urchins. They were carried back and forth helplessly until at last rescued, lacerated and almost drowned, green and blood-stained and shocked by so close a death.

3

Here comes the *meltemi*, carrying sand and papers, the dead surface of the desert through our houses. The dust-storm whirls among the trees of the little square beneath my window.

My friends, dear friends, I embrace you on the *agora*, in this splendid wind that cracks the electric awnings of the restaurants, in the dazing light so godlike-streaming from your faces.

Last week, the cranes passed very high overhead on their way to Africa.

4

On these fire-gleaming, passionate waters, it becomes clear how an experienced hero could demand of his sailors that they tie him to the mast in anticipation of the syren-call.

I sit close to Evangelos Limmiotis, both of us huddled against the spray, staring at the rain-speckled sea, or standing braced, as the boat cuts into the open swell.

Light-filled depths, full of sponges and squid, antique vases and bronze goddesses. At what are they smiling, those painted girls with the eyes of cats? And the youths, who yearn, blinded by salt, what do they desire?

La Mer! O Sea! thou Ocean, Thalassa! Indigo, green of jade, white, silver, black.

The island like a scroll unfurled to us, savage, more savage, green, orange pink, naked and crude, and under appalling cliffs, the musical movement of tall-masted fishing boats, weaving like dancers one against the other, with look-out men atop the masts.

The engines were slowed, and the heavy nets were drawn up slowly from the dyed and teeming depths. There were sudden squalls, savage salt-bursts of killing water, and the throb of our engine pulsed in the caves and against the rocks we passed near. And it is 'five years' since Michalis sounded his horn, and Leonidas stood up from beside a tree near the white chapel on the beach.

Already, these headlands are haunted for me with associations. There is to be no escape from the island.

Greece is a fighter's land.

At one moment, the fishing boats lay directly in our path, trolling swiftly upon the tracks of fish, but when we came up to where they should have been, the expanse of water was empty. The boats were in lee of a cove, at anchor, and the miraculous draught had begun to be drawn up from the translit water.

'To sleep in,' says the boatman, Evangelos Limmiotis, and it is a cave he points at, a long shallow niche made for siesta, a lair really, for a tawny beast.

I have a past here. Spring into summer into autumn. The cacti, when first I came, bore yellow flowers, and already I have eaten of their pulpy insipid fruits. Nostalgia for the past of only a few weeks ago? Yes, nostalgia for early mornings, the first days on the island, when from my bed I was able to look over cactus and boulder and white block of house, to the backbone of Ydra taking the first warmth on its flanks, and the sky was blue metal.

5

Pandora's box, the alabaster jar which was first opened for me in the nettle-bed and slate-fenced days of childhood in Wales to let out the Furies, is not forgotten, for now again the dreaded insects escape in a cloud when the lid is opened, to sting and blind and sting again. Behind the sun-soaked pillars and the classical sites and the caryatids swaying under the olive trees rise the Dirae screaming for vengeance.

Since childhood I have believed in the mask, the blood upon the steps, the chorus saying this is inevitable, these things are because they must be. It had served very well to have such things always at one remove, a cultural beauty, part of the background to life, but when it proved real in our time too, it stunned. In this world of violence and retribution I was seeking consolation from the Orthodox Church; no, that is not quite true, not only from the Greek Church, but from a belief in something beyond myself, call it God, the Cross, the Ever-virgin.

The world was after all still pagan and rooted in superstition. Determined to pit ourselves against it, Yanis and I went up the mountain at dusk to take part in the night-long vigil for the Saint's day of Efpraxia. What encirclings of hell we made in the darkness, locked away from one another in our minds, and yet with a common thought to bind us together—the agony of love, of how it can never be requited so long as it is temporal.

In daylight, the path up the mountain is difficult, but at night it becomes an enemy. There was a half-wish to give up, and lie down, or to go back home and sleep, but the collective will behind non-willingness forced us to go on in a kind of cursing silence. There

was no joy in it, never a more improper state of ungrace took feet on a pilgrimage. We were in a state of passion against the world, and our minds were heavy with thoughts of Leonidas, who yesterday left for Athens, and his trial.

On the stone bench outside the wide-open door of Efpraxia sat a man from the port, one of the town garbage-collectors, selling bottles of lemonade and orange juice, and packets of sweets.

Groups of townsfolk stood about the lower courtyard. The chapel, round which the pilgrims pressed with candles in outstretched hands, was filled with light and the sound of chanting.

One of the nuns came to me, saying,

'You have not eaten? You must come to the kitchen for food.'

We were given fish and salad and told that we could go to bed as soon as we had eaten, but I said no, we had come to take part in the vigil.

We took our places in the procession of candle-bearers, and entered the incensed air of the chapel, which was full of people. Some neighbours from the Kala Pigadhia cried out aloud when they saw me, and showed their pleasure by pulling me towards where they were standing. For hour after hour the chanting continued, the air became heavy with incense. At certain points in the ritual, the congregation streamed out of the chapel and circled the yard behind the priests. After we had walked thus, singing and talking, some of us arm in arm, the people formed an open circle round the priests, who held out for us the sacred relics. Early morning came, and the crowd thinned, melting away to bed in the cells and guest-rooms. A basket piled high with loaves of fresh bread was brought into the chapel and placed before the Royal door of the eikonostasion. The two doors on either side of this central door were open onto the 'Throne' where the oldest monk from Profitis Elias was struggling to change his vestments. I was becoming mesmerized by the rise and fall of the priests' voices. I felt that soon I should fall insensible to the floor of the sanctuary, so I went away through the open gateway and lay down under a tree on the breathing hillside, to wait for the virgin day.

I awakened to full light. Near me, two small birds were making love, hurling themselves at one another with open claws, vibrating awhile, then parting for further erotic flights among the flowers. There was an overpowering fragance of herbs. No other sound than the faint wing-clitter as the birds rose and fell.

6

A fight at Loulou's. An Asiatic type, smooth and brutal, a muscle-man from one of the caiques bringing grape-must to the island, was dancing with one of the tables held in his jaws, lifted from the floor by his teeth, wine-glasses and all. He was an old enemy of Yanis's, and later on, while they and other men were dancing an intricate movement, the muscle-man suddenly released Yanis so that he fell heavily on his hand. Abruptly, the dance stopped, the muscle-man threw down his komboloi in provocation, glasses were smashed, and the women at their table began to cry out on a high note to inflame the men further. By the time the police arrived, there was no sign of fighting. To our surprise, the table-lifter and his friends soon left the taverna, leaving us with a moral victory.

7

With a cable of vine tendrils, I anchor the ship of my heart to this comfortless island, like the small Ydriot seamen who were accustomed to moor their boats with twisted vine-stems, before they learned the use of steel cables.

8

Oh so hot, and the end of September! The fat little man, so happy, so successful an island business man, who had taken his first-born into Agios Konstantinos at nine o'clock in the morning for the child to light a candle (perhaps today, the man's wife will have her second child), having had his midday meal and being ready for siesta, and

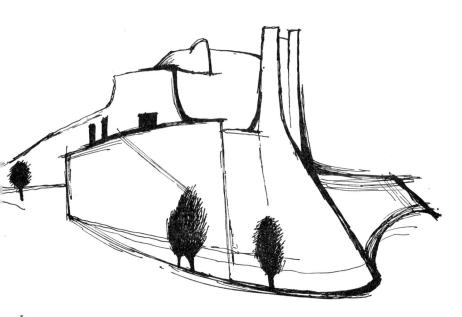

having put on his blue and white pyjama trousers and thick woollen vest to absorb the sweat, was suddenly filled with an aching thirst. Snatching up a bottle, he rushed down the steps, and eager for us to admire his *déshabillé* smiled down at his striped paunch and short legs. There was a roar from the men drinking outside Katsikas when he arrived in their midst, swinging the empty bottle by its neck.

9

Leonidas has been found guilty of manslaughter, and has been sentenced to imprisonment for nine months. He has sent me a letter, calm and cheerful on the surface, full of submerged tension.

He has written: 'The prison is a tall grey building on a hill, with a distant view of the sea.'

10

I cling to the evidences of Leonidas, to Varvara, to Leonidas's dog, to those who speak his name, to the sight of his handwriting, to Yanis, his friend.

I pray before the ikon, I pray for him when I am dressing in the morning, I pray for him as I am preparing to go to bed.

11

Every morning, before breakfast, I write a letter to my friend, in which I tell him of the small problems and happenings of the port and the *tavernas*, of how the season is slowly changing towards autumn.

Perhaps Leonidas is thinking:

'What is all this talk of the flowering desert, birdsong, nuns on donkeys? Why does she not write and tell me of what happened on the island at Election time?'

Yesterday, when the ship brought the newspapers with the result of the elections, there was excitement and exultation in the port, but no demonstrations of any sort. There was more a feeling of satisfied surprise than anything else, in this change of government, from Right-wing to the Democratic Party. Yanis thinks it will put a drag on the country becoming the complete police-state, but he was cautious and said, too truly, that men promise the earth in order to be elected, but after victory, who knows?

On the surface, everything is peaceful. The Marines, even the police, have melted away.

The most splendid caiques with proud inspired lines, are in harbour today.

12

For some years, I have been on the fringe of other people's lives. Now, on this island, I have found my way of life again, having my own table at Graphos', with my friends, my guests. I am sometimes in control of the situation. Often alas, the situation controls me. Before this eventful year in which, after so long, I have cut myself physically loose from my other island and an old pattern of being, I should have said it was totally unlike me to go into Graphos' *taverna* where they never sell coffee anyway, and to ask it as a special favour on a proscribed day, that of the Elections, but it was worth the danger, to see the pleasure of the two ancient campaigners in the sweet Turkish coffee served in fine cups. It is the weekend of the Greek General Elections, and no intoxicating liquor or coffee is to be sold in any public place from noon yesterday until Monday morning. Not remembering the proscription, Yanis ordered cognac last night, Saturday, at Douskos' *taverna*. Douskos said nothing, but brought the cognac in coffee cups. In a far corner of the bar, from his glass case, Napoleon, like a stuffed bird, watched us. In the opposite corner, a fisherman was smoking a nargileh.

Yanis and an old friend had been to the poll early. They were sitting in their best clothes in the port, enjoying the sun. Yanis seemed to be more than ordinarily pleased to see me. We wandered together up and down the port, through crowds of Ydriots returned from the mainland for the voting. The three of us were desperate for coffee; *Kyria* Graphos would surely help us. She said, yes of course, she would make some for us in the house. We slipped inside the door of the *taverna*, and Yanis' friend sat at the table in such a way that he could look out through a chink in the door, and he had a foot ready to hold the door from inside should anyone attempt to enter. However, we were in full view of anyone going up the steps outside the open window before which we were sitting, and a group of men stood there for some time, looking in at us suspiciously, but fortunately no policeman came past.

It was good coffee, full of sugar, and *Kyria* Graphos would take no money.

'The coffee is on the house.'

It was only at lunchtime that Yanis came out with what had been worrying him all morning. He had been accused of bribery when he was waiting to cast his vote!

Whilst standing in the queue, he had caught sight of his landlord, and without thinking, he took out money with which to pay his rent. A man saw him, told another man, who told Yanis,

'I accuse you of bribing the electors.'

Yanis, one of the saints of this world, to be charged with bribery and corruption—what a bitter joke.

Yanis' friend told me of how when he was travelling in Tibet in 1919, one of his porters called him out of his tent at dawn to see a Yeti.

'There was no time to put on my boots,' he said. The creature was silhouetted against rocks and sky, a naked hairy figure, bent over in the act of tearing up plants.

'My theory is that Yetis are descendants of penitents who took to the empty mountains of Tibet in contrition for grave sins they had committed, and that this was one of them, on the way back from man to ape.'

Is this then the ultimate conclusion of pushing the human spirit to its final bounds, that divinity is driven out, and the animal takes over? Man loses his clothes, grows hair in order to survive the great cold of the Himalayas, and learns which roots and berries will keep him from starvation. Is this the ultimate outcome of the struggle between the flesh and the prayer-wheel? Then again, it could be the perfect fusion of man and animal, pure spirit burning under shaggy eyebrows, and a fully awakened heart beating behind a pelted breast.

In the afternoon, escaping from the port, I went onto the mountain and sat on the side of the riverbed that in wet weather drains into the Kala Pigadhia. It was another Sunday, there was a woodpecker laughing at me in the boulders. Everywhere, small green plants had sprung up after the rains. I nibbled at the leaves, trying them for salad-flavour.

I am gnawed with worry for Yanis. I think to have discovered the man who accused him of passing money at the voting-room. He is one of the donkey men from the upper part of Ydra. He was watching us through the window outside Graphos' this morning as we were drinking our illegal coffee. This afternoon, as I was passing the Library where the men were casting their votes, I saw him talking to a policeman. He was shouting excitedly, and in mime, took a paper out of his pocket in the gesture of offering it.

'Dismal world,' you wrote. O miserable, dismal world of petty intrigue. This man is probably paying back an old grudge against Yanis.

The port is filled with Marines, with rifles at the ready. Marines with fixed bayonets outside the Library, Marines outside the Gymnasium, where the women are voting. There is an air of half-suppressed festivity, the peasant women are in high clackety heels and tight skirts. Lipstick, perfume, handbags.

Only ten minutes away from the port, in this belated Little Summer of Saint Demetrios, Adonis is ploughing red pockets of earth between rocks in steep, folded places of the upland.

It is a Turkish bath, the air. Swimming through thick silence, even the insects are dumb. I am looking up at our rock, the Koundaria, tranced in the oppressive heat. The mountain has reached its greatest point of aridity—it could not lie dead for ever—out of the utter sterility, the trees are green, the yellow-green of tenderest spring— and O my God, to break the heart on this day when already my breast is torn into a thousand pieces (still a cicada busy above me in the pines?) asphodel, asphodel, asphodel.

I like to have dirty feet, when it is red-earth dirt. I like to sit on the dust of the hill, and to let the living air wash over me.

I like to stare impertinently at lizards hanging under stones.

When I set out for the mountain, I was twitching and shaken with nerves, after the strain of spending a night in the ghost-ridden house, where I had gone to find certain papers Leonidas wished to have sent to him, and to water his orange and lemon trees; but now, having sat on the earth, and having looked and listened, having spoken with old neighbours, a beautiful woman and her small son who were taking out their goat onto the hill, I am calm again. I cling to the normal even if it is only a surface normality, to put as balance against the abnormality with which I am beset. For this is an island of terror, where no gentleness is, no cool glades in which to hide oneself away while wounds grow shining new skin.

Island, how long will it be before my heart bursts wide open at the hardness of you, your onslaught on my senses and affections, before the bitter drops of blood run out into the dust, you iron-bound savage island, Ydra-shale, on which plants and trees die in the nine-month drought?

I wish to pour away my wild blood, to become placid and ruminant.

Out of the red dust, rise up the wraiths of little dead nuns, asphodel. A remote thunder in the mountains.

A lotus-climate, with almost constant sunshine, does not necessarily make for happiness or health.

Leonidas's dog is with me and he is on his best behaviour. It is hot, hot, hot, with a clear heaven, and everywhere greenness.

My dear lame nun from Efpraxia went up her side of the mountain with three laden mules. She was riding a grey donkey, around whose behind was hung a bag to catch the dung.

At the side of the road was a squashed frog on its back, headless, with one hand raised in protest, the body covered in yellow fly-eggs. The nun's gentle donkey had trodden on it while descending the steps from the pavé. Wondering of what the raised hand reminded

137

me, I realized later in the evening that the frog's palm and fingers
had the same benedict-protestation as the left hand of the painted
Virgin on my ikon.

There was throaty bazouki-music coming out of a house near
Varvara's. She ran out after me, exclaiming,

'Oh, she knew at once it was Leonidas's dog, and remembered
having seen it with him the morning he passed on the way up to the
monasteri with my breakfast.'

A fine wind is coming out of the north, a few grasshoppers leap,
goatbells are sounding from the ravine below Profitis Elias.

Tonight, there will be a clear moon, judging by the afternoon sky.
This would be the day for going to Zourva, the unvisited monasteri in
the wilderness to the east.

I sit at sunny, sheltered corners, and write a few words. The dog
crouches very close, on the lookout for insects or eagles.

14

'A wind of so infinite a tenderness that she could not believe it to be
anything but miraculous made her pause and slowly turn her body
so as to receive its blessing on her hair, her throat, her legs, her eyes,
her breasts, the nipples of which were pressed hard against her blue
cotton dress. Instead of the sea-wind which had blown the island to
a hateful mood of violence, with policemen at every corner, and the
threat of police at the entrance to every passageway leading from
the port, the islanders filled with a latent violence, there had now
come after a day of intense heat this moist breath over the mountains
from the south and the new wind had, for the first time in months,
raised behind the cliffs a tall and ragged-edged grey cloud, above

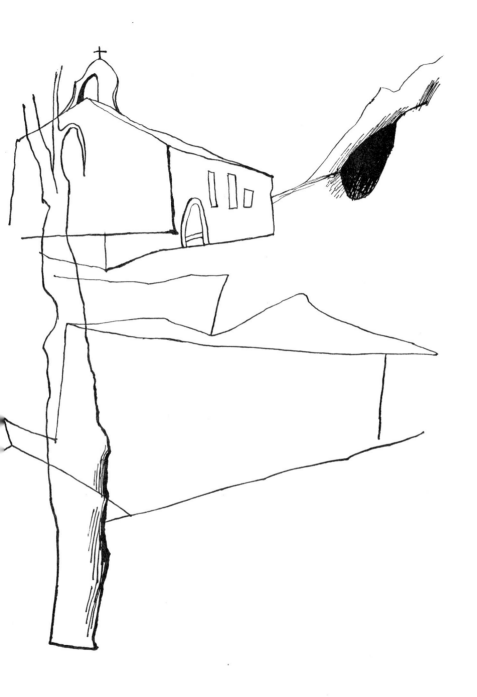

which a blurred moon was menaced by the same ragged edge suggesting a monstrous growth of trees. Faces softened, voices dropped, a dog barked at the moon.'

15

'This island burns me.'
A tree gold-weighed down with mandarin oranges, lemon trees. Goats on the rock, and a lame herd-boy playing for them on a flute. Already, we revel in the first sharpness of winter, in the juice of the pomegranate, in the first grass spread thinly over the land, the first flowers, a sun kindly to walk under.

16

'If half the town were to vanish in the darkness, it would not surprise me.' I should not be surprised if the whole island were to disappear. What I took for reality is a dream; the dream may decide to have substance.

This evening for example, when I had known him to be still in gaol, Leonidas appeared, a ghost on the *agora*. How had he come back to the island when there had been no ship? By *kaïki* from Poros?

The roaring of the sea is real enough, the screaming of the wind really does shake down the plaster from the ceiling. He told me once of his belief that there is something in the air of the island that causes tension, gives a sense of nightmare unreality. 'It is just the island,' he said.

His heart was broken when he had to leave it though he had often felt imprisoned by it, and had longed for somewhere less powerful

in which to live, for example, the next island, the elegiac Poros. Everything comes back to love or hate, to not being able to decide, once and for all, this I want, that I reject.

He used to say, it is because we are cooped up here between the sea and the mountains, trying to be artists, or pretending to be artists, exiles in a strong context, in an island too strong for most of us to fight against.

The Greeks do not give a damn for anyone, but there is Albanian blood here, and the people give less than a damn. We, the tender élite, feel ourselves menaced by small, sinewy men who spit with contempt for us.

17

I like the clangour of the monasteri bells. They toll, and the little churches clap in response, until a ring of praise reverberates the island. It is then the moment to press back the shutters against the whitewashed wall, and to lean over the music towards the harbour and the Gulf and the Peloponnesos and the further reaches of heaven, for it is a time of solemn joy, the ringing of the bells.

'. . . and in need of my prayers,' Leonidas's dog was with me, so I could not go into Agios Konstantinos, but prayed at home, and lit, for the second time today, a honey-candle. It was a beautiful morning of crisp wintriness.

The bells of the monasteri have been ringing and ringing at intervals since early morning for the feast day of Saint Demetrios. Why have I always, so far back as I can remember, hated the sound of English church bells, and yet fell in love at once with the chaotic clamour of Ydra bells—wild elation of frivolous notes behind solemn booms, joy and sorrow perfectly harmonized?

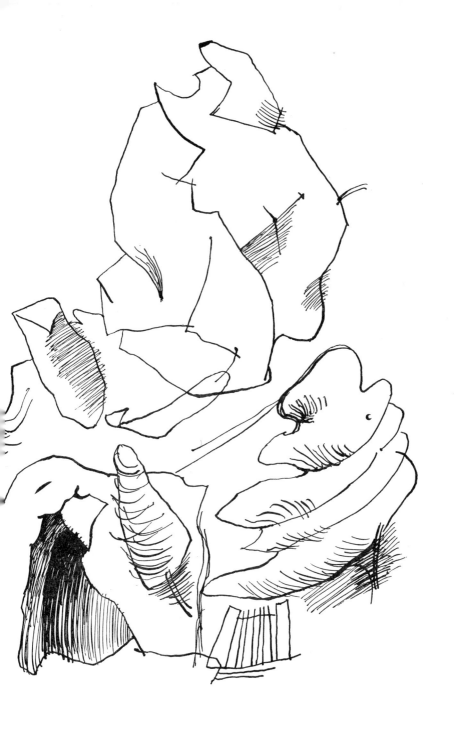

18

Leonidas once spoke about 'the descent from the mountain.' It is comparatively easy to endure the searing ecstasy of the rarefied peaks, very hard to accept the small pricks of daily life.

This is the most blessed time of my day, when I turn out of the port, away from the ravaging sea, into the *monasteri* to light a candle, a long one in the tall candlestick near the door; to tempt the wind, to take a gambler's chance of its being blown out or surviving, as a gauge to the day's fortune.

Saint Nikolaos, hope of seamen! The church is a shell full of dreadful waves, the chandeliers swing to the gusts and the silver boats suspended from the base of each respond to troubled currents of air as if they were not toys but rode restlessly in the troubled port.

Of what possible use, O my God, is this lighted taper? It is fragrant, soft, and sticky with bees' wax, and the cathedral is a cave to shelter the women who come in to pray for their men two years gone to ports foreign as Cardiff or Zanzibar, and I am wondering now, this short time later, whether the candle is still alight, whether a gust quenched it, or whether it has come to the end of itself in the natural manner, the wick lying dead on the heated brass.

Of what use are the strings and strings of *ex votos* of silver? Eyes, legs, crosses, arms, artificial flowers?

Each day, another candle is lit for a stranger. Every one of you is a stranger, friend, family, lover, enemy, acquaintance, behind the silver filigree and the golden ikons, rings, ribbons, silver legs.

The scent of honey from the taper fills the cool doorway of the *monasteri*.

All I am asking is a small victory over an evil fate, over a sort of death in life. Through this candle I fight a battle with myself, asking God to notice me and to give me respite and strength to front another day and to overcome another trial of endurance.

Rings, bracelets, crucifixes are bazaar-offerings in thanks to the Virgin.

What more can I do than pray, and light a candle every morning? Of course, I can do more for Leonidas than say my prayers and offer a lighted wax-taper each day. Something created as a gift, this book I can offer. For what, for whom do I pray? Is it for him alone, or for both of us alone or separate? For whom does the candle-flame shudder in the draught from the mountain? I wonder if he is protected by these things.

19

The grape-must used in the making of retsina has arrived from the mainland. The port smells rancid. Donkeys go laden from kaïki to warehouse, with the must in bloated goatskins. The men are black and greasy from carrying the tarred bladders to which the legs and hoofs are still attached.

20

The male islanders must spend a drunken winter, judging by the huge barrels that are being handled. The men are barefoot, lubricated, and happy as they sweat the barrels along the quayside and up the steps of the town.

Creaking of winches on the boats; mules under loads of lime and lengths of timber.

At night, the drunks go to be sick round the corner from Graphos'.

21

Ochimera OXI. In 1940, on the 28th of October at three o'clock in the morning, the Italian minister in Athens delivered to the Greek government an ultimatum, a demand for the surrender of the Greek forces. General Metaxas sent him the uncompromising reply, 'No.' Tubs of retsini, looking like pig-swill were lined up at the waterfront. Schoolchildren processed with flags as part of the celebrations, and the war veterans lunched together, with speeches, at Graphos'. Yanis's eyes were full of memories.

Helped with Popi's OXI for school tomorrow. The grandmother drew the letters on a sheet of cardboard, I drew a flag on a pole surmounted by a cross (like the one carried at the head of the procession this morning). The OXI and the flag were then pricked out with a needle, after which we took it in turns to stitch round the letters.

22

A party last night at Graphos' to 'celebrate the winter.' Graphos and his wife were back from a summer spent on the mainland, and as a result the cooking was amazingly improved, and everyone was in gay spirits once more. At one table, a party sang to the playing of the *santuri*. We killed seven bottles of red wine between us, two Greeks, two Canadians, and myself. I wondered how Leonidas was faring in Athens. We drank to his health.

They are spring-cleaning Graphos'! It is not the same place—so much water has been used, so clean a smell comes off the scrubbed tables. The walls have been whitewashed, the tables have been covered in new oilcloth. The pavement has been scoured of the summer's dirt.

Once more, it is outside weather, but the air is leaden. The walls are hot to the touch. The world smoulders, a cloud whitened by the moon, comes up behind the mountain. And yet it does not rain, though for several weeks now there have been clouds over the Peloponnesos. The sky becomes dense with moisture during the day but as night advances, the moon clears itself, Venus leaps the escarpment, and there is a sky of stars.

So many bats and so many shooting stars. On how many nights have we sat at Graphos', with the screaming cats and the dogs, spotted Ektor and the Man-dog, always on the perimeter of our table, in moonlight and in Venus-light, the white Cathedral and its campanile, and the man with ruined arms leaning to watch us from the parapet?

Stathos, the young attendant on the waiter, always on the run, an acolyte in soft shoes, is a radiant boy with smudges round his dark

eyes, and a pale sensitive face. His shoulders are hunched as though too much experience had already settled on his childish back.

They come off the sea in the rain-black night, the fisherman and his sons. The lads are dusky, with shaven heads, and they carry huge crusty loaves and strings of small fish which Graphos will cook for their supper. The barefoot father is a lion of a man, in loose home-spun trousers and a thick sweater. The young sons are uneasy on this island which is not their home. They crouch behind the father, pro-tected by his back, giggling, and glancing over their shoulders at the Ydriot men who sit, clicking their beads, bragging, and drinking.

23

In a letter to Leonidas, I have committed myself to saying, 'I believe in you.'

Does he realize how hard it is for me to say it? Those are words of commitment, like saying, 'I love you,' and meaning it, or 'I shall never leave you,' and meaning it.

It could be a bad omen to say such a thing, but on the other hand, perhaps it is just what he needs at this moment, for surely I am the only one who, at this juncture, sees him in a clear light, and can say, 'I believe in you.'

The island of decisions? There can be no half-measures on this rock, no poetic dreams. Leave before it is too late for recovery, or grit your teeth, clench your fists, and hang on to what the sea has to offer and to what the mountain holds out in promise.

There is a handful of people to hang onto for very life, but they too are leaving with the dying of the sun. With the first rains, they pack their bags and put on city clothes, becoming at once other people to us. As a parting gift, they are given a basket of mandarins fresh-plucked from the tree. From the upper deck of the white ship, they throw some of the bright fruit to us. What shall we do with ourselves, now that our friends have gone away? It is a good idea, to go onto the mountain, to gather wild geranium and to see how many different-patterned cyclamen leaves we can find under the trees near the white-washed mill.

24

A red-ochre kaïki, with pale-skinned, emaciated cattle aboard her, drifted slowly into the harbour, and was brought to berth at the waterfront where it had to stay for two days, with the cattle still aboard, the island butchers being slow to buy such thin beasts.

25

The land breathes out a scent of thyme. In this supernaturally warm weather, this summer in November, the jasmine is again in flower.

The house of Leonidas is shuttered, the door-knocker is unpolished, his house is abandoned, but from behind the high walls surrounding his garden comes the smell of jasmine.

I am uneasy on this side of the port under the split red rocks, and cannot walk any further, because I am half-blinded by the white glare from the steps.

When I arrived here, in what seems a lifetime away, I was reasonably detached, and could with an easy mind sit under a shade-tree to watch the reapers of corn, afterwards sharing bread and olives and cheese with them, taking part in the life of the earth, but on deeper issues unengaged.

To learn to be wiser through suffering, that is the kernel. What is the purpose of suffering, except to make us wiser? And disaster when it overtakes causes clarity of vision as if one were lifted high above the earth to see life in its perspective for a moment. The problem is

to remember the revelation, and not to be lost in the complicated cities of the plain. It is imperative to transform the dismal world and to turn the vision into a kind of sacrament. The alternative is to forget the event and the resultant suffering.

26

Sometimes, though not often, I wish I had a lot of money. Tonight, in a cold wind, sitting with Yanis, to warm ourselves we drank camomile tea laced with cognac. I should have liked to go out to the emporium, 'a thousand and one delights,' and return with a thick sweater and a tweed suit for him, but then, he would give them away to the first man he met. It warms one, to be in the company of a saint. He thinks only of other men's misfortunes, never of his own.

27

Night, and the first rains of the winter. The street past Graphos' was streaming with brown water, and children were playing in the flood. One of the men standing about told them to stop and go away, but they continued their wild games. The man lost his temper and knocked down one of the boys. A dense crowd from the port gathered in the narrow street. Men shouted, a woman screamed, arms waved.

Above it, rose the shrieks of the injured boy, who was eventually led away along the back of the cathedral. Supported by a man on either side, he limped past the table where I was eating my dinner. He wore the mask of tragedy, aloof in his dramatic pride, wounded perhaps, or dramatizing himself. He was my young friend Stathos, the child-attendant on the waiter at Graphos'.

Rain! As Leonidas had said they would be, in the hot weather when the possibility of a wet season seemed as remote as great riches, the streets are awash, a riverbed into the sea. A man fell on the steps at Graphos' because of the slime, there were vegetables running in the water, umbrellas were out, the din of water over human speech.

Despair! How far away he is, as in my dream, further than death. He is terrified, I am terrified too, of deprivation and self-discipline that goes so hardly against the grain. I am terrified by partings and by reunions.

I am afraid of the police-state, of ships with loudspeakers that come to tell the people the way they shall vote, I am made afraid by the fear of the people. At night, in the deserted port, the police are much in evidence.

We were peaceably eating our dinners at Graphos'. Two policemen came in, one behind the other. For whom were they looking? We were the guilty, we were ready to be led away and to be interrogated. We were guilty because we dared to be individuals, to be free to walk about. He flushed, the man at the next table, frowning in concentration at his plate. He hoped the policeman would not see how his hands were shaking. He was on bail, we were, every one of us, on bail for nameless crimes.

Here within the house-wall is security, down there is fear and honesty. I try to digest fear and honesty. From my neutral vantage-point, I can see the how and the why of human behaviour conditioned by local circumstance.

Let us say, there was a quiet, unnoticeable young man, small, thin, modest, an electrician. He had mild brown eyes and a thin moustache. He was a serious young man. One day, going to his work along

154

the cliffs near Kaminia, he stumbled over an object in his path, and picked it up. It was a foreign passport. Inside was a long book containing a hundred and fifty pounds' worth of traveller's cheques. He took his find home, and carefully copied the name from the passport, '————, ship's draughtsman, Glasgow, Scotland,' onto an envelope. Now he had to find the man who owned these things. His method was this. He began to ask foreign residents whom he could trust, if they knew the Scotsman. By chance, he came to Yanis and me as we were taking a coffee after dinner in a *kafeneion*. We denied any knowledge of the name, being put off by bafflement at the empty envelope. As he walked away, I remembered it was the name of the man on furlough from Hong Kong, and he and his wife and child were still in a rented house up the Kala Pigadhia. The electrician looked happy at this. But what would he do now? Would he take the mysterious envelope to the owner?

The next night, by pure chance, because Yanis and other friends were performing a beautiful slow dance with handkerchiefs with two fishermen at the time I passed by, I went into Loulou's, and saw that the ship's draughtsman was sitting at Yanis's table. I told him about the mystery of the envelope, and he was intensely interested, and thought it must have something to do with his affairs. The young man was not at Loulou's, and I forgot about it.

The next evening, after the exhaustion of great rains throughout the day, the people drifted into the damp aftermath, among silt and debris in the port. Yanis and I were drinking cognac outside Katzikas, and the electrician was at the next table. The Scotsman was standing at the other side of the road and was plainly concentrating on me. I hunched my shoulders defensively. He came up and said, 'Brenda, I must speak with you. It may be very important. About this envelope, I think it could have something to do with my passport.'

I looked around, the young man had disappeared.

'He was here a moment ago. Let us look for him.' We went into the *kafeneion*. He was at the far end of the room, talking with friends.

'This is the man whose name you have put on the envelope.'
The Scotsman began to get excited, he said he must have an interpreter. Yanis was now go-between.
'I must bring my Greek friend Apostolis,' said the Scotsman.
'What about the money in the passport?'
'There was no money.'
'He is entitled to ten per cent reward,' cried the Scot.
'Easy, easy,' said Yanis, 'these people are not to be insulted.'
'Why did he not take the passport to the police?' asked the foreigner.
'Because he did not want to be beaten up,' was the reply. A port trouble-maker who never misses anything if he can help it, now sidled up and was about to get involved. This was the time for us to withdraw. We left them still talking it over, the young electrician going home to fetch the passport and the cheques.

28

I do not think so much about his house as of the rock-bastion behind it, grey and red and implacable. Leonidas is not like rock, but is nonetheless part of it. His austerity and fanaticism owes something to stone.

He has said he needs a lot of time in which to be alone, but I do not believe the truth of that statement. Though he dislikes people, he seems to have a nervous compulsion towards them. I really do like to spend a large part of my days alone. Solitude is necessary to me, so that I can hear the earth breathing. The voices of men and women dement me after a time. I prefer the sound of goatbells in the distance. And light shining through a snail-shell.

Against the secret smile, the covert glance, the crucifying word, O God, give me back my innocence. Let me be honest in the market-place, let me wear my own face, not the mask others would have me wear.

When no more suffering throws me then I shall be dead.

In wind and rain among the ruins, donkeys and their dirt, among thistles and cacti, amongst dreary shuttered and secretive houses newly seen in this wet weather, it was misery and fearfulness to stumble.

Why should it be that the children I know are so friendly and full of gifts of flowers to me, while these few urchins I encountered among the stones on the other side of town ran after me begging for two drachmas? I was shocked and angered, and wondered why the children should have been corrupted in this far distant corner of the labyrinth.

On this wet tail of afternoon, the corruption of the year stalked me. It was the first time since the two drunken men chased me at night on the Kala Pigadhia that I have known panic in this town. I wanted to bang on all the shutters, to beat the doors, to get human beings out into the wind and rain. It was the dead end of day.

29

Night on the *agora*, in the rain, walking damp and tired over the treacherous deserted paving. Who dances, along the length of the port?

The downpour of the past few days has entered deeply into my body, making the muscles of my neck and shoulders ache with rheumatism. My feet and legs are now always damp and cold.

I surprise myself. What are these shapes dancing along the length of the port? They are caiques, with painted poops and heroic tillers, surreal, unreal, vessels my imagination has dredged up; and why should not the squat wooden hulks with swaying masts that rise questing into the darkness speak for me, for mankind, for the sieved seas and the thymy mountains. They join the sky to the earth by stretching their yards heavenward, and by grinding their bows

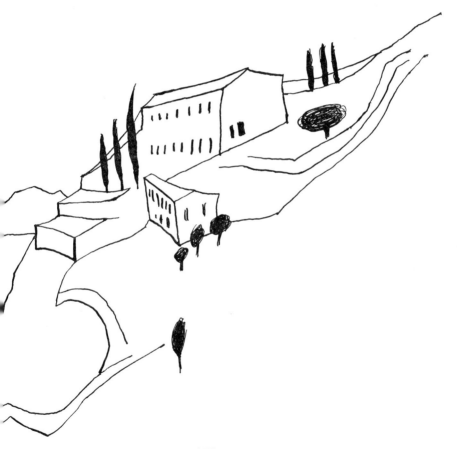

against the stubborn rocks of the quayside. Now at midnight, they snore fast asleep at their wheezing chains. Stray dogs bark in the far reaches of the port.

It has begun, with pluckings at the sky, fistfuls of air drawn on an O of breath. The earth has need of the energy of man's nostrils, the black sky is grasped at, the yard-arms creak, the stars are scythed, a god is being invoked. The tall masts sprout green leaves. The god and the identifying vessels fuse.

We invent our own lives, but there remains reality outside oneself, and these enduring boats, laden with melons and water pots, green peppers, and cattle, point the way to life through abundant dying.